TOOLBOX NO. 1
USING VISITATION TO SUPPORT PERMANENCY

TOOLBOXES FOR PERMANENCY

by Lois E. Wright

CWLA Press • Washington, DC

CWLA Press is an imprint of the Child Welfare League of America. The Child Welfare League of America (CWLA) is the nation's oldest and largest membership-based child welfare organization. We are committed to engaging people everywhere in promoting the well-being of children, youth, and their families, and protecting every child from harm.

CHILD WELFARE LEAGUE OF AMERICA, INC.
HEADQUARTERS
440 First Street NW, Third Floor, Washington, DC 20001-2085
E-mail: books@cwla.org

CURRENT PRINTING (last digit)
10 9 8 7 6 5 4 3 2 1

Cover design by Tung Mullen
Text design by Michelle Peña, Capitol Publishing Corporation

Printed in the United States of America

ISBN # 0-87868-808-0

Library of Congress Cataloging-in-Publication Data
Wright, Lois, 1942-
    Toolbox No. 1: using visitation to support permanency / by Lois E. Wright.
        p. cm.
    Includes bibliographical references.
    ISBN 0-87868-808-0
    1. Foster children--United States--Family relationships. 2. Visitation rights (Domestic relations)--United States. 3. Child welfare--United States. 4. Family social work--United States. I. Title.

HV881.W75 2001
362.73'3'0973--dc21
                                                                            00-0666091

Contents

Tables

Figure

Acknowledgments

This publication could not have been written without the dedication and assistance of many people. Pamela Day, director of Child Welfare Services, Child Welfare League of America (CWLA), provided ongoing coordination of the project. Kathy Barbell, formerly director of Family Foster Care, CWLA (currently director of the Casey National Center for Resource Family Support), carefully read drafts and offered helpful suggestions, always with an eye toward the realities of practice. Sarah B. Greenblatt, director, National Resource Center for Foster Care and Permanency Planning, kept the faith throughout, with her commitment to permanency and her bone-deep valuing of maintaining connections. Lucy Salcido Carter, program officer, The David and Lucile Packard Foundation, understood not only the importance of bringing people together to discuss promising practices but also the necessity for providing follow-up in the form of toolboxes to put information in the hands of practitioners. My editor, Michelle Peña, was a joy to work with as she helped me clarify ideas and tidy up wayward sentences. Last, people too numerous to name spent time discussing various ideas with me, always providing a valuable perspective on visitation and how it is experienced by all parties involved in this most critical aspect of child welfare practice. I wish to thank all of these people for having made this publication possible.

Introduction

Toolbox No. 1: Using Visitation to Support Permanency* is intended to assist child welfare staff as they confront how best to plan and implement visits between parents and their children in out-of-home care to achieve permanency goals. This publication contains helpful aides (or "tools") that practitioners can use quickly and easily to guide their thinking, and it offers much information to support use of these tools. Our thinking is that, although the tools are helpful quick-reference guides, they can be used meaningfully only when they are fully understood. Thus, the tools should serve as reminders of what one knows in greater depth; they are not a shortcut to knowledge.

Why a publication on visitation now? Permanency planning has been a central focus of child welfare since at least 1980 when The Adoption Assistance and Child Welfare Act (PL 96–272) articulated a hierarchy of permanency goals—maintaining children in their homes, reunification, adoption, or another permanency option. Child welfare experienced beginning success under this legislation, before certain challenges—increasing child poverty, overrepresentation of children of color, an influx of infants and toddlers, increasing numbers of children with emotional and behavioral problems, increasing numbers of children affected by HIV or AIDS, and the pervasiveness of substance abuse—began to erode our progress (Barbell & Wright, 1999). Permanency planning seemed to have lost its steam, as old methods were inadequate in the face of new problems.

The Adoption and Safe Families Act of 1997 (ASFA, PL l05–89) reaffirmed the importance of permanency planning, but in a very different way. PL 96–272 had suffered some criticism, rightly or wrongly, that it overemphasized reunification at the expense of child safety. In response to this, ASFA clearly articulated that child safety was always the primary concern. In addition, it emphasized moving quickly toward permanence by setting new timelines for both determining and achieving the permanency plan. The legislation encouraged concurrent planning as a method for hastening permanency decisionmaking when reunification looks questionable. In other words, rather than moving through the permanency options in a sequential fashion, practitioners could be working simultaneously on both reunification and another alternative such as adoption in certain cases.

Perhaps the new requirements of ASFA were not as different from earlier requirements as was the philosophy ASFA seemed to support. Just as the strong permanency planning philosophy behind PL 96–272 may have led some practitioners to overemphasize reunification at the expense of safety, it was possible that the ASFA emphasis on timelines and concurrent planning would lead to precipitous termination of parental rights (TPR) and adoption. Surely the effect of any new legislation goes beyond the letter of the law to how people perceive it and how they behave in response to their perceptions.

Both the meaning of ASFA and how to implement it in light of best practice have been broadly discussed among practitioners, policymakers, judges, advocates, and others involved in child welfare. Among those groups interested in how ASFA would be carried out were the Child Welfare League of America (CWLA) and the National Resource Center for Foster Care and Permanency Planning (NRCFCPP) at the Hunter College School of Social Work, which joined to initiate a project aimed at assisting jurisdictions with implementation. They entitled their initiative "Renewing Our Commitment to Permanency for Children," communicating that permanency planning needed to be revisited and reinvigorated under the new federal requirements. The initiative sponsored a series of activities, including

■ a launching conference (funded by the Johnson Foundation) at Wingspread that reviewed what had been learned about permanency planning over the past two decades and described successful permanency outcomes for children and families in current practice;

■ a series of regional practice forums (funded by The David and Lucille Packard Foundation, The Casey Family Program, and the Jessie Ball duPont Fund) for discussion of successful permanency outcomes and best practice strategies and formulation of action plans;

■ onsite consultation and technical assistance; and

■ creation of a series of Tools for Permanency publications (of which this, *The Visitation Toolbox: A Practical Guide for Using Visitation to Support Permanency,* is one).

This publication presents the best professional child welfare practice in relation to visitation, within the context of current federal legislation. We realize that some agencies are already implementing much of what is described here. Yet most will identify areas in which practice can be improved. Of course, we all work under the tensions of time and resources and best practice. Still, without a vision of best practice, we have little hope of moving forward, at whatever pace we can, to continually improve our practice and to improve children's chances for safety, permanency, and well-being.

Defining Visitation

This chapter will explore the full meaning of visitation in the context of child welfare services. It will offer a brief definition of visitation, elaborate on the definition, establish visitation in the context of case planning, and examine visitation in the context of various case goals.

What Is Visitation?

Visitation is generally defined as planned, face-to-face contact between a child (or children) in out-of-home care and his or her biological (or created, as through adoption) family, apart from family counseling (Chiancone,1997). It has been described as the key to successful reunification (Loar, 1998) and the heart of reunification services (Hess & Proch, 1993). Visitation is the primary mechanism through which family relationships are maintained while a child is in out-of-home care. In addition, it provides the context for learning if and when a parent is willing and able to provide a safe environment for a child or if a permanent plan other than reunification is to be considered.

In the context of this publication, visitation does not refer to the child welfare worker's contacts with the parent, child, or foster family, though these contacts provide essential supports for visitation (e.g., previsit and postvisit sessions with participants) and though the worker as well as others may be present at the parent and child visitation. In addition, though visitation between a child and a noncustodial parent is an important service in relation to divorce (and the literature on divorce has much to lend to our understanding of child welfare visitation), the focus here is on visitation as a child welfare service—a service offered when children have been removed from their homes through the child welfare agency, usually due to abuse or neglect.

Visitation Fully Understood

Two recent and related developments in visitation have broadened our understanding of what this service can and should be. The first development is an *ecological approach* to visitation, reflecting our understanding of ecological child welfare practice in general; and the second is the use of *team approaches* to visitation. Both trends are reflected in such practices as family decisionmaking and family conferencing.

Ecological practice may be defined as practice that considers children and families in the broader context of their environments. It recognizes that families do not live in isolation and that family functioning can be supported or endangered by a variety of contextual factors—extended family, fictive kin and friendship circles, neighborhood, community (including formal and informal services), and society.

In terms of visitation, an ecological approach enables us to understand that children in care are separated from more than their parents (Oysterman & Benbenishty, 1992). Typically, they are also separated from

- siblings, other relatives, friends, and pets;
- school, church, and possibly other associations; and
- special places or things—not only their own room and possessions but also the park, the corner drug store, or their favorite fast-food restaurant.

Thus, visitation fully understood includes keeping children connected to a range of family members and other important figures in their lives and to their immediate neighborhoods, supporting rather than undermining their sense of belonging, offering ongoing reassurance and reinforcement of the continuity of place and social networks (Millham, Bullock, Hosie, & Haak, 1986).

Just as the ecological approach to visitation reflects the direction of child welfare practice in general, the team approach is evident today in all of child welfare practice. Certainly there is no one model of teamwork, but generally it involves a variety of professionals and non-professionals with defined roles, working together in common purpose toward a case goal. In terms of visitation, the core of this team includes the parent, child, foster parent(s), and worker. Newer expanded approaches may include not only other important people from the child's ecology (e.g., extended family, friends) but also additional service providers, particularly when visitation services are provided by a private agency or in demonstration projects or special-focused programs. These others may be, for instance, specially trained visitation observers, parenting teachers or role models, or neighborhood resource workers.

Thus, visitation may no longer be thought of as exclusively parent–child contact (though that remains the core) but rather as enhanced by broader, well-coordinated efforts to better meet the attachment and connectedness needs of children and their families, as well as to support parenting and case decisionmaking.

Visitation and Case Planning

Although visitation is the primary factor influencing reunification (Chiancone, 1997; Hess, 1999), the primary context for determining when a child cannot return home, and a primary issue in family case plans and court orders, it is not an isolated service or stand-alone intervention. Rather, it is part of the *larger case plan* (Hess & Proch, 1993).

Thus, it is important to remember that visitation must mesh with other services that are part of the case plan. These other services may include such things as counseling for a child, regular contact with the child's school, psychological counseling for the parent, parenting education or training, or addictions counseling. Whatever the mix of services, they converge around visitation. It is during actual parent–child contact that the effectiveness of these other services is put to the test. The only assurance that the services are resolving the family problem(s) that necessitated placement is to be found in an extended period of well-documented, face-to-face parent–child contact in which the parent demonstrates an increased ability and willingness to parent the child safely. Likewise, the best way to document that the parent cannot or will not parent the child safely and that another permanent plan is required is through such well-documented, face-to-face parent–child contact.

Visitation and Case Goals

Traditionally, visitation has been viewed as a service in support of reunification. But this exclusive focus must be broadened to include other case goals. As we understand more about the lifelong significance of family connection, even when the parent and child must be permanently separated as in adoption, the importance of visitation regardless of the case goal is highlighted. In addition, the increased use of a broad variety of arrangements between children and parents, and thus a variety of case goals other than reunification and traditional adoption (e.g., formal and informal kinship care, guardianship, open adoption, long-term foster care), impel us to consider how visitation can best support child safety, permanency, and well-being within each of these options. Generally, we aim toward maximal links and connections between the child and family regardless of the case goal, unless this is strongly contraindicated.

Last, the practice of *concurrent planning*, in which the understanding from the beginning of placement is that the case goal can change (e.g., from reunification to adoption), emphasizes the utility of visitation not only in supporting more than one case goal but also in determining the most appropriate goal.

Summary

The traditional child welfare service of visitation continues to be the heart of reunification services (Hess & Proch, 1993). In addition, our understanding of this service has broadened to include ecological thinking and teamwork; and visitation is understood as part of a well-integrated case plan and is supportive of the variety of case goals.

Why Visitation
Is Important

Though visitation is important for many reasons, a primary one is to preserve and strengthen the relationship between children in out-of-home care and their parents and other people who are significant in their lives (as well as familiar places and things). When the state uses its authority to remove children from their home we must remember that, though the removal is necessary to protect children from abuse or neglect, it exposes them to a new danger—the emotional, mental, and developmental harm that may be associated with separation. Visitation is a service that can mitigate the harm inherent in separating children from their parents and other loved ones.

This chapter will look at the impact of separation of children from their families and the importance of maintaining linkages. It will also look at visitation as a child welfare service, listing a range of benefits that include but go beyond maintaining relationships.

The Impact of Separation

Our understanding of the impact of separation on a child is based primarily on attachment theory, which, though still equivocal, forms the basis of current child welfare practice. Drawing on psychoanalytic theory and specifically the work of Ainsworth and of Schaffer and Emerson, Bowlby (1969) described a process by which an infant, by age four months, begins to show a marked preference for its mother as compared to other people and exhibits behaviors (e.g., crying, following with eyes) to signal that preference and to remain in close proximity to the mother. We call this preference and the associated behaviors "attachment." The child tends to show this strong attachment to the mother through the third year of life. By that time, though, the child begins to generalize attachment and is better able to feel secure with other attachment figures, such as relatives and family friends. Attachment behaviors in a child of this age are still present but less urgent than in the infant.

Attachment behaviors continue even through adolescence and adult life, though they are apt to become increasingly generalized, directed toward not only people outside the home but also groups and institutions. Bowlby notes that attachment behavior in adults is a continuation of childhood attachment behavior and that under stressful situations, adults intensify their attachment behaviors, looking for the known and trusted person. He also underscores the strong emotional impact of attachment and states that any threat of loss of attachment figures creates anxiety, sorrow, and other intense feelings (Bowlby, 1969). Subsequent writers (Falberg, 1979; Jenkins & Norman, 1972) have continued to document the importance of maintaining and strengthening attachments, particularly in relation to children in the child welfare system.

Thus, attachment may be understood as an affectional bond that originates with early mother-figure/child proximity and interaction, is signaled by a variety of behaviors, becomes more generalized as a child matures, endures throughout life, and when frustrated causes distress. Within this understanding of attachment, it is clear that separation of children from their parent(s) through an event such as out-of-home placement can be a severe threat to attachment and can cause severe distress.

Millham et al. (1986) and Hess and Proch (1993) have pointed out the *ubiquitousness of separation,* which we all experience throughout various periods in our lives, and the types of separation from loved ones to whom we are attached. Certainly many families experience separations through such things as military service, other extended work assignments, hospitalizations, divorce, or death. Such separations, whether brief or for extended periods, always involve some feeling of loss, and we all draw on various strategies for coping with and lessening the pain. Most of us, unless we have had significant trauma around attachment and separation in our pasts, take these separations in stride and tolerate them reasonably well (if not always happily).

Separation from family and other loved ones is particularly difficult for children for several reasons. First, their *understanding of time* (depending on age) adds an additional burden in that they are less able than adults to understand when the separation will end; to a very young child, the pain of separation seems to have no end. Second, children are less able to tolerate the separation; they have *less well-developed coping strategies* than adults. Last, they are usually less able than adults to comprehend the reasons for the separation. In addition, when the separation is due to extreme family disruption, as is often the case when there is abuse or neglect, all family members are adversely affected and *adults in the family may be unable to offer the support* the child needs to weather the emotionally charged events that seem beyond the control of both the parents and child (Millham et al., 1986).

Two common types of separation involving family breakdown are divorce and out-of-home placement of a child in foster care, most likely associated with child maltreatment. Though the focus of this work is separation due to out-of-home placement of a child, Wallerstein and Kelly's (1980) extensive clinical research on divorce tells us so much about how children react to separation from a parent through divorce that it merits attention. Particularly valuable is the age breakdown, highlighting how children at various life stages react differentially, based primarily on their ability to comprehend events and the range and maturity of their coping strategies. Thus, the following material draws heavily upon their work as presented in the valuable book, *Surviving the Breakup: How Children and Parents Cope with Divorce.*

Separation and Infants

Because infancy is the critical period during which attachment develops, children separated from their primary caregivers during the first two years of life are particularly vulnerable to disturbed attachment relationships. Disruptions in attachment may occur for a variety of reasons. The caregiver may be physically present but psychologically unavailable, as in instances of maternal depression, substance involvement, or reactions to a child characteristic (e.g., disability, temperament). On the other hand, the caregiver may be physically absent, as in instances of divorce, death, incarceration, serious illness, or child out-of-home placement. Whatever the reason for the separation, it leaves the infant extremely vulnerable and unprotected and usually has lifelong consequences, including a range of attachment disorders (e.g., unattached, insecurely attached, anxiously attached).

Separation and Young Children

Young children (aged 3 to 5 years) have little cognitive understanding of the events around separation, have trouble sorting out fantasy from reality, and have only the most immature coping strategies. Children of this age group who are separated from their parents typically experience deep pain (though Wallerstein and Kelly [1980] noted that some very young children in their study managed to cope well in the face of parental divorce, maintained their balance, and reestablished some sense of order within their disrupted lives). Typical reactions to separation for children of this age group include the following:

- *Fear*—expressed as clinging and whimpering, and anxiety, which peaks at bedtime.

- *Regression*—returning to behaviors more typical of an earlier developmental period (e.g., returning to security blankets or outgrown toys or showing lapses in toilet training), marking time or moving backwards to regain strength.

- *Fantasy*—used to explain events that are beyond their understanding. Because the child cannot comprehend actual events or explanations of events, or in the absence of explanations of events, she may provide fantasy explanations that often are vastly off-target. Fantasy may take the form of total denial of events or may involve unlikely scenarios of family restoration (going home) or replaceability (creating a new family).

- *Guilt*—false ideas that the loss was somehow the child's fault. Children may believe it was their bad behavior that caused them to be ejected from the family.

- *Bewilderment*—total inability to comprehend the loss, and forthrightly expressed pain. Children's confidence in human relationships may be so shaken that they express their loss primarily through aimless searching for the absent parent whom they so sorely miss.

- *Changes in level of aggression*—either rising aggression or inhibition in aggression.

- *Generalized emotional neediness*—looking for affection and physical contact anywhere they can find it, reaching out to strangers.

- *Play*—inability to enjoy play and using play to recreate the family.

Separation and Early School-Aged Children

Early school-aged children (aged 6 to 8 years) have the cognitive maturation to grasp some events, have a beginning understanding of cause and effect, and can begin to understand the meaning of those events for them. Though their sense of time is still immature, it is more realistic than that of younger children. They do, for instance, understand how long a week is and can grasp waiting periods between visitations. Their involvement in the world beyond that of the family, such as school and peers, provides some additional support. Early school-aged children are apt to show the following reactions to separation:

- Limited use of fantasy and denial, and pain and sorrow that is experienced at a more conscious level.

- Limited fantasies of responsibility and deep wishes for reconciliation.

- Grief and pervasive sadness often expressed through unrelenting crying and sobbing. The impact of the separation is so strong that their usual defenses and coping strategies cannot hold sufficiently under stress.

- Fear of being left without a family, leading to disorganization and panic.

- Feelings of deprivation and wondering how the necessities of life (e.g., food or toys) will be provided. These feelings may be expressed as compulsive overeating or begging and manipulating for gifts and other concrete signs that they will be cared for in a material sense.
- Lack of concentration and inability to enjoy tasks, as yearning for the parent takes precedence over all else.

Separation and Preteens

As children reach their preteen years (aged 9 to 12 years) they show an enhanced capacity to understand reality, which includes understanding the meaning of events for them. This better grasp of reality can be sobering. On the other hand, they also have an improved capacity to withstand stress, using newly developed coping skills rather than the more primitive defense of regression. Wallerstein and Kelly (1980) found that preteens could actively and valiantly struggle to master the new events and emotions in their lives. Preteens were apt to show the following responses to separation:

- Layering and cycling of responses. As they actively work through a variety of age-appropriate coping options, preteens may alternatively reach for cognitive mastery of events, retreat into refusal to believe or into distraction, engage others for support, and exhibit bravado or real courage. But at other times they still may exhibit real distress.

- Participation in a variety of activities as a mechanism for overcoming feelings of powerlessness.

- Anger, sometimes quite intense, expressed as both an honest reaction to what is happening to them and as an externalizing attempt to cope with their pain, sadness, and helplessness.

- Shaken sense of identity, as the foundation meant to support the preteen's identity formation and eventual launching is threatened.

- Moral lapses, as the foundation of development of morality (parent) is shaken and the child experiences painful injustices, evidenced in such behavior as lying and stealing.

- Somatization, with symptoms such as headaches and stomachaches.

Separation and Adolescents

The reaction of adolescents (aged 13 to 18) to separation is clearly related to their primary developmental tasks of identity formation and launching into adulthood and to the extensions and intensifications of processes beginning to be evident in the preteen group. The normal struggle for independence shows a backwards and forwards motion, with parents alternatively vilified and praised, rejected and depended on, and the adolescent alternatively showing signs of maturity and independence and childishness and dependence. Removal from the family during adolescence derails this process, and the adolescent's development may be fast-forwarded (leaving the age-appropriate tasks poorly completed) or halted. At the same time, the adolescent is experiencing strong and unfamiliar sexual and aggressive impulses. Cognitive understanding of the separation is greatly matured, issues of right and wrong are prominent in the adolescent's mind, and emotions can be overwhelming. The adolescent experiencing separation is apt to show the following reactions:

■ Mourning the loss of home and family. Symptoms of mourning may include such things as feelings of emptiness, tearfulness, difficulty concentrating, chronic fatigue, and troublesome dreams.

■ Anger, both as a direct response to disruption and circumstances surrounding it and to cover feelings of powerlessness, vulnerability, and grief.

■ Withdrawal, both psychological and physical distancing and detachment. Adolescents, because of their greater independence, mobility, and access to resources (e.g., friends, organizations) outside the home, are often able to withdraw from the problems of the home to maintain their equilibrium.

■ Periods of failure to cope, as defenses wax and wane. Developmental regression, evidenced as choosing younger friends, withdrawing, interrupted school achievement.

■ Social and behavioral problems, such as sexual misconduct, truancy, delinquency, substance abuse, and gang activity (Johnson, 1992).

Additional Considerations

The previous text alerts us as to what reactions we may see in children experiencing separation. Yet, any one child may exhibit few or many of the anticipated reactions for his or her age. The following caveats are important considerations in understanding some of the differences we may see among children:

■ *Separation is always traumatic for children*

Regardless of the cause of or circumstances surrounding the separation, it has a profound effect on children. Although much of the information provided above is based on clinical research with children experiencing family break-up through divorce, there are many similarities with out-of-home placement. Possible areas of difference are that in divorce the child is usually still living with one parent and often in his or her own home and neighborhood; and that children in the child welfare system are more apt to have experienced the multiple traumas of poverty, ongoing family disorganization, and maltreatment.

■ *A child's reaction to separation is partly dependent on the quality of attachments*

Not all children are similarly attached to their mothers or other figures. Children who have experienced severe neglect may, for instance, be only weakly attached. Such children may show minimal reaction specifically to separation, yet they show ongoing difficulties in close relationships and may be very challenging to parent. Other children, perhaps those for whom emotional closeness and abuse co-occur, may be anxiously attached and show exaggerated symptoms upon separation.

■ **Children's responses to separation will vary according to their developmental level**

It is the specific tasks, cognitive abilities, and coping abilities of each stage that give rise to particular reactions. Children in the child welfare system often have experienced multiple and ongoing trauma that leaves them developmentally below age level. Thus, their reactions to separation may resemble those of children from a lower chronological age group.

■ **Uncertainty hampers a child's ability to cope**

Although coping with known bad situations is difficult, coping with uncertainty is even more difficult. Yet, uncertainty pervades the child's life when she experiences out-of-home placement. Answers to such questions as "Where will I live?, Who will care for me?, When will I see my parent again?, When will I return home?, and What will happen?" next remain nebulous. The child enters a period of remarkable instability and uncertainty, not even knowing with what she must cope. The more uncertainty— due to unavailability of facts, lack of communication, or limitations in ability to comprehend—the greater the difficulty in coping.

■ **Trauma diverts children from developmental tasks**

It is normally expected that children's emotional energy will be invested in mastering their age-specific developmental tasks (i.e., forming attachments and developing trust, developing autonomy, developing initiative, learning to work productively, and achieving identity). The everyday challenges children experience, if they have the coping resources to meet them, make the children stronger and move them forward developmentally. But if the challenges are too great and exceed children's capacity to cope, emotional survival begins to take precedence over mastery of developmental tasks, and they begin to show developmental delays (e.g., retarded language development) or regression (e.g., soiling or clinging) as well as other inappropriate coping strategies (e.g., numbing) (Wright 2000). Thus, in understanding children's reaction to the trauma of separation, we must look not only at the more obvious direct responses but also at how the diversion of energy affects overall development.

■ **Children's reactions will vary over time**

Although we lack sufficient longitudinal studies documenting how children's reactions change over time, we know generally that a crisis reaction is different from a long-term accommodation (adaptive or maladaptive) to trauma. In addition, we know that intervention is more effective if it is offered before maladaptive patterns have settled in and begun to feel "normal" for the child. Theory related to the grieving process suggests that people go through stages of grieving. Although the pattern of reaction is not invariable and the theory not entirely substantiated, it does provide some guidelines for understanding changing reactions over time.

Having reviewed the trauma of separation and how children may react, we now focus on how we as child welfare professionals can help them through this trauma.

Maintaining Linkages

Separation due to out-of-home placement can be so traumatic for children that, if the child welfare system is to "first do no harm," it has a sacred responsibility to ease the pain associated with separation as well as to help children progress along their developmental paths and to return them to safety and stability as soon as possible. These things are best accomplished when we ensure that linkages between children and their families (and other aspects of "home") are maintained throughout placement.

As already shown, separations occur for all of us throughout life. And normally, we ease the pain of separation through various strategies aimed at maintaining linkages, keeping the absent loved ones alive in our minds and hearts. Millham et al. (1986, p. 98) points out the normal strategies we use for maintaining connections with loved ones when we are separated: "In daily life we give little thought to the complex process by which we maintain contact with family, kin, and friends. We reach for the telephone, gossip with our families, remind our children of mother's birthday, and annually make out a list of Christmas cards without the guidance of a sociometric test....even the shortest separations can add a problematic dimension to maintaining links with our families and inject unfamiliar anxiety....Indeed it takes much effort to maintain links with the separated, in which time and money, energy and inclination, are prerequisites."

Children in out-of-home care are much more vulnerable than are most of us experiencing our normal separations. They have no control over the separation, it occurs amid trauma, they have limited information about or understanding of the separation, and being children they lack control of the resources for maintaining contact. Because maintaining contact can be so emotionally and logistically difficult for all parties, linkages tend to wither over time if they are not specifically supported and encouraged (Millham et al., 1986). It is thus up to us, the professionals and other helpers serving children and families, to ensure that connections are maintained. Through us, those important linkages will either be encouraged and maintained or allowed to wither (Millham et al. 1986). Though it may be enhanced by other mechanisms (e.g., telephone calls, letters, e-mails, celebrations, and memories), visitation is the core service for maintaining connections.

Visitation as a Child Welfare Service

On the psychological level, visitation has been considered the most important service for maintaining connections between child and family and thus for easing the pain of separation. Yet it also serves broader related purposes for the child welfare system.

Purpose

Visitation is a service designed to achieve a certain purpose, which may also be stated as an outcome. This is actually the same purpose and outcome that child welfare services in general are to achieve. Thus, the purpose of visitation is

- to effectively achieve the case goal or permanency planning goal for a family, while

- promoting child safety, permanency, and well-being.

In addition, visitation has been found to increase the likelihood of reunification, usually the preferred permanency plan if it is consistent with child safety, and to reduce the length of time in care (Hess, 1999), always important but even more so in terms of the Adoption and Safe Families Act time limits.

Benefits

Visitation is the unique service that best supports achievement of the purpose stated above, and it does so through offering a range of benefits. Remember that involuntary removal of a child from his or her parent's home is an undesirable (usually) but necessary action to protect a child from harm. Visitation is the primary mechanism for healing the parent–child breach caused by both the maltreatment and the separation; and for building or restoring a home for the child that provides safety, permanency, and well-being. It is unlikely that these things could be achieved outside the context of parent–child contact, guided and enhanced by a skilled worker and skilled foster parents. All other services for parents and children who have been separated through out-of-home placement may be seen as augmenting the benefits of visitation.

The following list of benefits of visitation is an expansion of information that appears in a variety of sources (Chiancone 1997; Loar 1998; Hess 1999; Hess & Proch 1993; Warsh, Maluccio, & Pine 1994). Visitation has been shown to

- ***Ease the pain of separation and loss for all***

    The pain of separation is often repressed and comes out through a variety of symptoms. Visitation helps both the parent and child express and deal with this pain (Littner, 1975).

■ **Maintain and strengthen family relationships**

Links between child, parent, siblings, and other important figures must be maintained, regardless of the case goal.

■ **Reassure the child of the parent's well-being**

When the parent and child are separated, the child does not know what has happened to the parent or how the parent is doing and will naturally be concerned. Visitation lets the child see that the parent is all right.

■ **Deal with changing relationships and support the family in coping with changes**

Throughout placement, family relationships will shift for a variety of reasons. A new member may enter or leave the parental home, or the placement itself will cause relationships to shift. These need to be recognized and dealt with on an ongoing basis.

■ **Enhance parental motivation to change through providing reassurance and hope**

The parent's motivation to change will be enhanced when ongoing contact with the child provides reassurance that she is still the parent and will continue to have a meaningful role in the child's life.

■ **Enhance parental empowerment**

Millham et al. (1986) observed that parenting has a power dimension. Normally parents have some power to affect their child's lives, and children enjoy the sense that there is a loving parent who can look out for them and intervene on their behalf. This power relationship is greatly eroded when a child is in care, but visitation can be used to enhance it.

■ **Provide the opportunity for parental change**

Visitation provides the setting in which parents can learn new behaviors and can practice, rehearse, and demonstrate that they are making progress in the areas of parenting related to the reason for placement.

■ **Help participants deal with reality**

We have seen that there is much fantasy and distortion (due to defenses as well as lack of information) when children are in care. Regular parent–child contact combats this problem and moves participants toward a better grasp of and ability to deal with reality.

■ *Support the child's adjustment in the foster home*

Children show fewer behavior problems when they have regular visitation, which helps them cope with their pain and can also allow the parent to give permission for them to settle in.

■ *Provide the context for self-assessment and agency assessment*

The parent needs to assess how the child is doing, and the agency needs to assess the parent's ability to provide a safe home for the child. Visitation is thus essential; it provides a face-to-face opportunity for the parent to demonstrate this ability.

■ *Support decisionmaking*

Visitation provides the opportunity for observation of the parent and child in a variety of settings that will clarify parenting competencies and thus support decisionmaking regarding the case plan—whether it can continue as reunification or must be modified.

■ *Reduce time in care*

Regular visitation has been shown to support reduced time in out-of-home care (Hess, 1999).

■ *Increase the likelihood of reunification*

Regular visitation has been shown to increase the likelihood of reunification after out-of-home care (Hess, 1999).

■ *Assist with transition to reunification*

Families need a period of transition from out-of-home care to reunification. Progressively increasing the frequency and length of visits, decreasing and eliminat ing supervision, and moving to overnight and extended visits in the parent's home allows for a gradual resumption of responsibility and opportunity to identify and resolve problems.

■ *Contribute to family stability once reunification has occurred*

Visitation can reduce the likelihood of disruption after reunification has occurred (Simms & Bolden, 1991).

■ ***Provide the forum for ongoing information sharing***

Visitation provides a regular time that parent, child, and other significant participants can meet for ongoing information exchange about the child, family, progress, and any changes that affect the child and family.

■ ***Enable the parent to stay current with the child's development and activities***

The child's life goes on while she is in care, and it is important that the period of out-of-home care not create a huge gap in the parent's ongoing knowledge of the child. The parent needs to know when the child cuts a tooth, takes a first step, has a first date, or joins the church choir.

■ ***Support child developmental progression***

Much child development proceeds best within the context of a permanent and loving relationship. Thus, it is important that the parent continue to be present to help the child along in his or her developmental progression. Continuing parental contact is fundamental to the child's sense of self, significance, and identity (Colon, 1978; Cantos, Gries, & Slis, 1997).

■ ***If reunification is not the plan, help participants cope with another plan, grieve, and work out their future relationship***

Regardless of the case plan, visitation will help the family transition to their new realities.

■ ***Provide the material needed for accurate, verifiable documentation***

The worker will need to prepare written documentation to support any recommendations in relation to the child and family. Visitation is the worker's best source of information for documentation to support decision-making.

Conclusion

We have seen how devastating separation can be for children and the variety of reactions they may experience. It is up to child welfare professionals to recognize these reactions and to support children and their families as they live through their trauma, and visitation is the primary mechanism through which they fulfill these responsibilities.

Yet, visitation is a complex and difficult process. We are reminded by Millham et al. (1986) that visitation requires of parents much social skill, as they experience rolelessness, are discouraged by reactions they do not understand, find the structured setting embarrassing and artificial, and "perform" what should be a normal life task under the scrutiny of professionals. It is no wonder that, despite their best intentions, parents sometimes begin to let visits slide. It is up to child welfare professionals to support them and all participants so that this does not happen. It is too important to be left to chance.

The General Experience of Visitation

We have defined visitation as an important child welfare service, and we have built a context for examining it based on the meaning of separation of children from their parents and other meaningful figures, as well as the significance of maintaining links with those who are important in children's lives. We have also established the complexity of visitation in consideration of the range of attachments that children have to people, places, and all else that comprises what is familiar and comforting to them, and the deep yet poorly understood psychological processes that are aroused when such attachments are threatened.

This chapter will continue to build our understanding of visitation by examining the general experience of visitation as it is felt by the primary participants—the parent, child, foster parents, and service providers. Although the descriptions certainly will not fit any one situation perfectly, because each family and situation is unique, they are meant to provide an overview of what participants might experience and a background against which we may interpret what we see and hear from specific parents, children, and other participants.

Visitation Is a Cooperative Venture

All participants have a special role and responsibility for ensuring that visits are productive. This requires not only that participants gain an understanding of their own reactions but also that they correctly interpret the reactions of other participants. Thus, we might think of the information provided in this chapter as supporting the development of a complex web of empathy among all parties that will enable service providers to use visitation in the most sensitive, humanistic, and effective manner toward achieving case goals with all families.

Figure 1 depicts a framework for understanding the complexity of visitation in terms of participants and processes. All participants—parents, children, foster parents, service providers, and others—simultaneously pass through a process in which each visitation event may be seen as occurring within a larger context of separation (through placement) and resolution (through either reunification or another permanency outcome). The entire process of visitation within the context of the case plan may be conceptualized as having three stages—early, middle, and late—each with its own tasks and character. In addition, each visitation event follows a three-part cycle, both temporal and emotional, of anticipation, the visit, and aftermath. Participants experience this cycle repeatedly. How well they progress through each visitation cycle, and how they build and learn as they progress through the stages of visitation, will greatly influence the eventual resolution to the initial separation.

Figure 1: Visitation Cycle—Participants and Processes

STAGES and EVENTS

Early	Middle	Late
Antic/Visit/After Antic/Visit/After	Antic/Visit/After Antic/Visit/After	Antic/Visit/After

Participants

Parent

Child

Foster Parent

Service Provider

Others

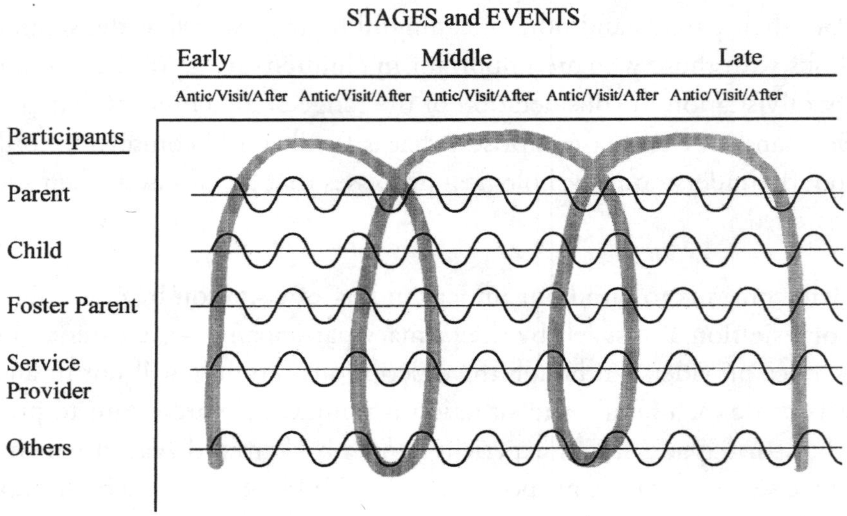

The following text examines the thoughts, issues, feelings, and resulting behaviors of the parent, child, foster parents, worker, and others as they experience the visitation cycle of anticipation of the visit, the visit itself, and aftermath of the visit. It is important to remember that, because each visitation event is a reenactment of earlier reunions and separations (Hess 1999), reactions tend to mimic original separation reactions. For example, a child with a history of traumatic disruptions in the parent–child relationship will feel that trauma repeated when she enters foster care. The reunion with the parent during visitation may then feel quite desperate, as the child anticipates, based on past experience, that it will only lead to another traumatic separation. Without appropriate intervention with the child, each visitation will replay this scenario.

The visitation experience changes throughout the placement period. Both the emotions and the tasks associated with each stage change, as participants move from the initial visit to achievement of the permanency plan.

■ Early visitation is characterized by emotional upheaval. Feelings are raw, understanding of events is minimal, and coping strategies are not yet established.

■ During the middle period, emotions will have settled to some extent, accommodations will have been found, and parties will focus on the tasks at hand.

■ Finally, during the later period, when consolidation of gains and concentration on tasks related to reunification or another permanency option are paramount, new emotions, related to the next transition, will begin to surface.

Close attention must be paid to participants' thoughts and feelings throughout all stages of visitation. Yet, because understanding and effectively handling those thoughts and feelings during the first few visits is critical to the entire visitation process, the focus of this discussion will be on the early stages (those visits immediately following placement and in the next few weeks).

Parent

The first visit (which should occur within the first week of placement) comes on the heels of events that have disrupted family life, undermined parental authority, and put the entire family on the road of events of which they have little understanding and over which they have little control. The last time the parent saw the child might have been when the child was forcibly removed from the home in an emergency protective custody action, perhaps under chaotic circumstances; it might have been in the cold and threatening environment of the court; or it might have been within the context of finally packing up a few belongings of the child as he was taken away after a failed attempt at in-home services. Whatever the circumstances, the last contact was riddled with pain and uncertainty. It is extremely important that the *healing process* for both the parent and child begin immediately. Amid the trauma, space must be made for the parent's strengths to emerge and flourish.

Thus, with the first visit, the parent begins seeing the child under an entirely different set of circumstances from those of the separation, circumstances that carry the pain of the past but also a promise of hope for the future. How might the parent anticipate the visit? How will the reality of the visit be experienced? And what might the parent feel, think, and do after the visit?

Anticipation

Before the visit actually occurs, as soon as there is any discussion of a visit, the parent begins to have thoughts and feelings about it and begins in some way to prepare for it. In so doing, the parent first confronts a medley of feelings that combine emotional reactions to actual events and defenses against those reactions. In addition to the pervasive pain and sadness related to the separation, the parent may experience other emotions. For instance, the parent may feel shame and embarrassment at her parenting failure. The parent may also feel shame and embarrassment at being labeled as inadequate in front of not only the child but also usually other family members, friends, and neighbors. (The removal of a child from home is seldom a private event.) Last, the undermining of parental authority that is implicit when the state forcibly intervenes in family life brings its own shame and embarrassment. The parent may also experience guilt, as she sees the breakup of the family and the pain that this has caused the child and understands that these things are the result of parental acts of omission or commission. Guilt may be particularly intense if the parent also feels some relief and thankfulness that the child has been placed (Horejsi et al., 1981). These emotions may combine to form depression, which can seriously inhibit the parent's ability to function adequately in the process of visitation that has been designed to resolve the family crisis.

Anger may be a direct response to the event. The parent may be realistically angry at whoever reported the abuse or neglect that led to the child's being removed, at the worker and the agency for interfering with family life, at the court, or at others she sees as involved in the removal of the child.

But the anger may also be a defensive reaction. During this phase one task for the parent is to hold herself together emotionally. Thus, when pain and self-recriminating emotions are so strong that they threaten to overwhelm, an unconscious process of calling defenses into play is a natural response; other emotions that are more acceptable to the psyche are substituted for the less acceptable emotions. Typical defensive reactions may include denial, in which the parent acts as though there is no problem or minimizes the problem; numbing, in which the parent is unable to feel anything; or rationalization, looking for ways to explain what is happening that do not incriminate the parent.

Within all these feelings there is also ambivalence. Although the parent longs to visit the child, she may also dread the encounter, not knowing what it will be like or what will follow.

In addition to dealing with this medley of feelings, the parent must deal with real concerns about the child. Regardless of the quality of parenting she is providing, in the parent's mind she has loved and cared for the child as nobody else could. How could strangers know the child's favorite foods, how the child acts when he is sick, or the bedtime tucking-in rituals? How could the child not feel absolutely bereft?

But even this concern about the child is fraught with ambivalence. Even though the parent wants the child to be doing well, is that not an indictment on the parent herself? While it is painful for the parent to believe that the child misses her, the parent may also wonder, "What if the child doesn't miss me?" Would that not be even more painful for the parent? And what if the child is doing better in foster care than at home? Thus, the parent's wish for the best for the child is tainted by fears concerning her own parenting abilities. The parent may simultaneously want to hear the child say he is doing well and that the foster home is terrible and the foster parents are mean. Having suffered a terrible narcissistic blow at the removal of the child, the parent cannot tolerate another blow due to feeling inferior to the foster parents.

Last, the parent has concerns about how the anticipated visit will go. There is great uncertainty about the visit. The place may be strange or may be familiar, but the process will certainly be one for which the parent has no model. In the absence of real information, and in an attempt to make sense of and gain some control over the situation, the parent will begin to fill in the blanks with fantasy. The parent will build a mental representation—a picture in her head—of what the visit will be like. The parent will visualize greeting the child, how the child looks, the child's reaction to her, the conversation, and activities. The mental representation may incorporate many of the parent's fears, such as whether the child will blame the parent for the separation, if the child truly misses the parent, or how the parent will handle the child's pain. The parent may have concerns about the questions the child will ask, particularly about returning home, and may have prepared responses. On the other hand, the mental representation may be highly idealized, including only a fairy-tale picture of the perfect reunion.

Thus, the parent anticipates the first visit with a confusing medley of emotions, concerns, and questions; and all is marked by uncertainty. And however the parent has anticipated the visit, whatever the mental representation, it will be at least partially wrong. The only questions are how wrong will it be, and how will the parent handle it?

The Visit

Depending on an array of factors, including particulars associated with each family and situation, conditions of the visit will vary in terms of such things as where the visit occurs, who is present, how long the visit will be, whether it is supervised, and the complex interactions that occur as one person acts and another reacts. Whatever the situation, though, the first visit presents an enormous emotional hurdle. Negotiating it successfully is a challenge, as expectations and fantasies, hopes and fears, meet reality head-on.

Many elements of the first visit would suggest it is a recipe for disaster; thus, it is important to remember that without assistance from the worker or another source, it may be just that for the parent as well as for others concerned. Emotions are raw. The parent will carry a mental picture of the visit that is bound to be shattered. Uncertainty is high. And the sheer newness of the situation, lack of adequate models of behavior to guide the parent, and unnaturalness of the setting for parent–child interaction result in extreme awkwardness. Add to this that the parent has not yet had the time and experience to develop the coping strategies that will enable later visits to go more smoothly, and one begins to appreciate the immensity of the demand that is made on the visiting parent.

The visit may be conceptualized as involving first the initial encounter, then spending time together, and last saying goodbye. The parent wants the child to come to her arms and for everything to be all right again, but this will not happen. First, the parent is awash in the confusing emotions that were present in the anticipation phase—pain, ambivalence, and happiness at seeing the child, mixed with the shame and guilt that she cannot take the child home (Beyer 1999a). These feelings will be not well focused and the parent is vulnerable.

Next, seeing the child may arouse more longing than it satisfies, deepening and widening the hole in the heart rather than filling it; and the parent may be totally unprepared for this reaction. Last, communication will be complicated by the enormous emotions in both the parent and child, resulting in complex interactive layers of misunderstandings and hurts. For instance, if the parent has defended herself by numbing, the child may read this as rejection and defensively reject the parent. Or the child may from his or her own pain exhibit numbness or hostility, anger or depression, leaving the parent feeling rejected—certainly not what was in the parent's mental picture of this coming together. On the other hand, a child's clinging and crying may devastate the parent even further, calling all the guilt and shame to the surface.

After the initial meeting, the parent and child have the task of filling time together. This will usually be at least an hour and possibly longer. But in any case it will be an awkward, circumscribed period of time for the parent and child to spend together, always watching the clock and amid enormous emotional tension. The parent will probably feel some defensiveness about her own parenting, may be resentful at her lack of control of the visiting situation, may feel competitive with the foster parents, and may let her own needs interfere with focusing the visit on the child. Adding to the tension and awkwardness is that the parent knows she is on display for "the system" (Beyer 1999a). Thus, the parent's own emotions may erupt in uncontrollable tears or anger or, to ease the difficulties of the situation, the parent may arrive "self-medicated" with alcohol or drugs (Beyer, 1999a). Unfortunately, either of these could necessitate cessation of the visit.

Often during the visit a parent is able to show real affection for the child, as well as attempting to reclaim him, through such activities as fixing the child's hair, arranging clothes, teasing, cuddling, and using familiar nicknames. If the child has changed during the period of separation—new hairdo, new clothing, new toys—the reclaiming behavior may be particularly obvious, as the parent attempts to eradicate the influences of the new "parent" on the child and reassert her own parental authority.

Finally, it is time to say good-bye. This is an extremely awkward period. The child may have believed he was going home with the parent, and the parent will have to deal with this disappointment. Both the parent and child may cling, expressing and exacerbating one another's pain; or they may be nonemotional, again expressing (defensively) and exacerbating pain. All the feelings of the original separation are aroused.

In all likelihood, time both dragged and flew during the visit. It dragged in relation to such things as the dread of what the child might ask, trying to make a very unnatural situation feel natural, or dealing with a child's negative reactions. Yet at the end, knowing that it was too late to change anything that might have gone wrong and that it would be a period of time before the next visit, everything that was unsaid or not done rushes into prominence; but there is no time for tidying up all the loose ends. The final leave-taking must always feel premature.

Aftermath

A visitation event is not over at the conclusion of the visit. Rather, there is considerable aftermath: *emotions,* already high, have been further aroused. While there is some satisfaction at having seen the child, there is also disappointment in how the visit fell short of expectations, specific hurtful aspects of the visit, or the inadequacy of the time spent together. The parent will mentally relive the initial separation and reexperience the loss and grief. The parent may also play and replay her mental tape of the visit—what actually happened, the meaning of the child's words and behaviors, what the parent might have done or said, and how the visit might have been different.

The parent needs to "come down" emotionally from this first visit before the next visitation event and return to the anticipation stage. In addition, how well the parent processes information regarding this initial visit will greatly influence subsequent visits. It will influence whether the parent meets the next visit with distortions and misunderstandings, leading further away from reality and productive visitation, or if the parent has learned something about herself and the child and faces the next visit with more realistic expectations and enhanced control of self and the situation.

Child

Like the parent, the child experiences the first visit after placement amid events that threw the family into crisis, events over which the family, and certainly the child, have little control. In fact, the placed child is apt to be the participant feeling most helpless and manipulated by events. For one thing, though good practice demands that the child be involved (as is age-appropriate) in planning, in reality—because of such things as caseload demands, lack of appreciation for a child's needs for information and input, and some workers' lack of skill in communicating with the child—the child is often left on the fringes of planning, which is seen as an adult affair, or given information in a perfunctory way that may fall short of fostering understanding or real involvement.

We have seen earlier how a child's reaction to separation is age-related. The same is true of visitation. How a very young child can understand, respond to, and shape events is very different from how an older child or adolescent can be involved. Although we will not attempt here to fully analyze child reactions by age, some reference to age is necessary.

Anticipation

At the time of placement the child (old enough to understand language) should be told when he will next see the parent. Although this generally should be within the first week, for some young children it may need to be sooner. But it is important to remember that simply giving a child the words about what will happen and when may not communicate the concepts accurately. For instance, while an older child may hear and understand that the parent will visit next Tuesday, the very young child may hear the words but continue to think he will see the parent that evening; when evening comes and the parent does not arrive, the child is in anguish.

Thus, very young children, with their immature grasp of events and immature sense of time, after being away from home for perhaps a week will tend to react to separation with *bewilderment.* They have little ability to understand or to process information about the separation or about the visit, so for them the anticipation is only an unfulfilled and perpetually disappointed longing.

Early school children have a better understanding of time, and telling them that they will see their parent within a week has some meaning. They are apt to feel primarily a deep yearning for the parent. In addition, they may have fantasies about the visit that include going home with the parent that day. Still, at that age the child's understanding of time and events, though better than that of the younger child, is immature to the extent that it is difficult to help the early school child understand the limitations of the visit and that it is only one event in a series that will go on for some months.

Older children and adolescents may be particularly insulted if they are not consulted about the scheduling of visits. They have their own social calendars and expect these to be respected. Thus, consulting them in planning visits can forestall some of their feelings of powerlessness (Wallerstein & Kelly, 1980). In addition, since older children and adolescents understand time more as adults do and have more cognitive understanding of events, they will know that the visit is only a visit, not a return home. This higher level of understanding, while protecting them from the utter bewilderment experienced by very young children and forthright yearning of early school children, requires them to design coping strategies so they can handle their greater understanding. This greatly complicates their reactions. Thus, as they struggle to cope with (and mask) the sorrow, their surface emotions and behavior may include such things as anger, a blasé attitude, or seeming disinterested in the visit.

The Visit

Whatever else a child may be experiencing or expressing, he will be happy and relieved to see the parent (Beyer, 1999a). Whether the child be very young and unable to fully anticipate the visit or older and looking forward to it, the visit is a climax after a period of waiting. The visit will not only provide the emotional relief the child so longs for but also, for older children, assure them that the parent is all right and calm their worries about the family.

Yet there may be great ambivalence, as the happiness and relief are adulterated with other confused feelings. The child will continue to be sad and perhaps (for older children) angry about the separation; may be angry at the parent for the maltreatment that caused the separation; may be fearful of the parent in relation to earlier maltreatment; particularly for younger children, may be confused at the conclusion of the visit when he is not able to go home with the parent; may feel resentful at the loss of control, particularly if the visit was planned without consulting the child; and may feel guilty that he might have been responsible for the separation (Beyer, 1999a).

In addition, the child will be dealing with loyalty issues. Even adult professionals have trouble conceptualizing the "acceptable" emotional place of the foster parent vis-a-vis the biological parent in the child's life. We used to tell foster parents that they were to be as a parent to the child; but more recently, in light of revised ideas of the function of out-of-home care and permanency planning, we have conceptualized their role as supporting rather than supplanting the biological-parent role. What this means in terms of a child's feelings for, attachment to, and understanding of foster parents is still not clear. So it is not surprising that the child will feel confused and torn as he juggles the two relationships. How and whether he can like the foster parents without being disloyal to the biological parent is a puzzling emotional dilemma.

As in the anticipation phase, reactions and behaviors during the actual visit are age-related. During the visit younger children are more apt to show their pain through clinging and crying, whereas older children and adolescents are more apt to hide their pain through various defensive maneuvers—anger, disinterest, or withdrawal. Children of any age may attempt to extract gifts from the parent as reassurance and to soothe their pain. Generally, some behavioral difficulties are the norm, as children of whatever age struggle to cope with a sea of emotions that are difficult to understand and difficult to communicate.

It is important to remember that, as with parents, children's reactions are part of complex interactions: how they react to the visit is partially shaped by circumstances of the visit, what the parent brings, and how the parent reacts to the child's reactions and attempts to express himself, however veiled the communication.

For instance, just as the child may appear strange to the parent, the parent may appear strange to the child. This may be due to the physical setting of the visit if it is unfamiliar, because we tend to experience people contextually. (Even as adults we might fail to recognize people out of context, as when we see our doctor in the grocery store and know there is something familiar about her but just cannot place the face.) It may be due to the artificiality of the visit, as the parent struggles to interact with the child under the scrutiny of the agency in a particular place and a truncated timeframe. It may be due to the parent's own depression or struggles with her own concerns, which interferes with normal parental interactions. Or the parent may be under the influence of substances taken to numb the pain. All these factors add to the strangeness, which can confuse and dismay particularly the very young child.

The child will also react strongly to any failure on the part of the parent to comply with the plans for the visit. Tardiness, failure to show, or unkept promises are clear evidence to the child, not able to understand the logistical and emotional difficulties of the parent in making visits, of rejection.

How the parent responds to the child's attempts to express himself will be particularly influential in shaping the child's further reactions. If the child's acting out is seen only as bad behavior and withdrawal seen only as rejection, the parent's defensive reactions are apt to come into play, pushing the child further away and leaving him feeling even more confused, hurt, and defenseless. In addition, if the parent attempts to soothe the child with false promises (e.g., about the next visit, gifts, quick return home), the effects on future visits is devastating.

At the end of the visit, saying good-bye is as hard for the child as for the parent; and, like the parent, the child experiences it as a reenactment of the initial separation. The crying and clinging of the younger child might intensify; the early school-aged child may be confused and dismayed that he is not going home; and the older child and adolescent may steel himself against the pain by further withdrawal, rejecting before he is rejected. The visit needs to end with the promise of the next visit, but the child's ability to understand that is age-related.

Aftermath

During the visit a child's emotions will have been enormously aroused, and this state of high arousal will continue in the foster home. Not only will emotions about the initial separation be re-aroused, but the disappointment of unfulfilled fantasy (returning home) and dashed expectations will exacerbate the pain. For all children and particularly the younger ones, a behavioral reaction to the visit may be expected, ranging from somatization to acting out. Older children may deny that the visit was meaningful while showing their confusion behaviorally. Due to age-related limitations in understanding and communication and the flood of confusing emotions associated with the visit, no child is able to adequately express verbally what this experience has meant.

The extent of the behavioral reaction is related not only to the child's age but also to the overall cognitive and emotional developmental level of the child (which may be significantly below age-expected developmental level) and his adjustment to the foster home.

The aftermath of the visit is a particularly critical time for the child and for the future of visitation. First, in response to the painful feelings the child is experiencing, he may try to extinguish any further desire for contact with the parent, particularly if the visit went badly. Or he may have an intensified longing for the parent to heal the further hurt. Second, the child's expression of his pain through such things as regression (e.g., babyish behavior, demanding behavior, fearfulness, whining, wetting), depression, somatization (physical symptoms), numbing or denying, nightmares, or acting out (behavioral problems such as irritability, aggression, over-activity, inattention, or school problems) may be viewed by the foster parents and others in the child's life as problems resulting from the visit and as indications that visits are not good for the child and should be discontinued (Beyer, 1999a).

There is also danger that the foster parent will interpret these expressions of pain as resulting from something the biological parent did to the child. In this case, the foster parent may criticize the biological parent, adding to the child's feelings of guilt and defensiveness for the family. As the time of the next visit approaches, these same reactions may be reexperienced in the next anticipation phase.

Foster Parents

For foster parents the visitation experience is different from the experiences of the biological parent and child, because foster parents have not gone through the same trauma of separation and grief. For them the experience is more apt to be related to perceptions and feelings about themselves as foster parents, perceptions of the biological parent, and issues around the child's experience of visitation. Generally, differences among foster parents in their understanding of participants' emotions, ability to accommodate the inevitable disruption that visitation can cause, and ability to participate in helping the parent and child capitalize on the healing and growth-producing aspects of visitation relate to their experience as foster parents, skill level, training, and other agency supports.

Anticipation

As with other participants, foster parents may feel some ambivalence as they anticipate the first visit after placement. Particularly if they are experienced foster parents, they will understand the importance of the visit but also may experience some dread.

The foster parent may wonder how she will be viewed by the parent. She may take special pains about the child's appearance to reassure the parent that the child is being well cared for (which may also add to the sense of strangeness for the parent if the child looks too different). The foster parent may also wonder how she will be portrayed by the child. What will the child say about the foster parents? These concerns can produce some anticipatory anxiety.

Foster parents vary greatly in the role they assume in terms of preparing the child for the visit. Some may do little, whereas others (with greater experience, training, and other supports) are quite skilled to giving the child information and preparing the child emotionally.

Foster parents will always have perceptions, notions, and feelings about the biological parent that will influence what they communicate to the child about the visit. Although the agency will have provided them with some information about the parent and the child's maltreatment, that information will be incomplete. Thus, foster parents are apt to wonder about many things: Who is this person from whose home the child had to be removed? What did she do to the child that necessitated removal? What kind of parent could have done these things? Does the parent love the child? Can the parent be trusted to visit without further harming the child psychologically if not physically? Foster parents vary greatly (again, relating to experience, training, and supports) in terms of their understanding of these questions and of possible answers. Some will find it hard to forgive the parent for harming the child, whereas others may be very empathetic. Some will understand that the parent can love the child but still have parenting deficits, whereas others may see loving and hurting as incompatible. New foster parents, who have not yet experienced a birth parent's growth and eventual reunification, may find it more difficult than will experienced foster parents to be empathetic toward the birth parent.

The foster parent will hope that the child feels reassured by seeing his parent (Beyer, 1999a). Yet, because she has lived with the child through anticipation of the visit and sees the child's pain and confusion, the foster parent may be concerned. The experienced foster parent anticipates the emotional upheaval that the visit will incite and may dread this disruption and consequently dread the visit itself. The foster parent may believe that the child is just beginning to settle into the home and thus may resent the "step backwards" that she anticipates will result from the visit. Thus, the foster parent, like other participants, may be ambivalent. She may want to support the visit but still may find it difficult to do so honestly and wholeheartedly. Again, the more experienced foster parent is more apt to understand the importance of visitation, despite difficulties, and to understand that positive change can and will occur.

The Visit

The foster parent may or may not be present during the visit, and the visit may even take place in the foster home. If she is present, there will be a specific role to fulfill (e.g., supervising, modeling, teaching), and the foster parent should have received some preparation for that role. Still, the foster parent may struggle to be supportive of the biological parent if she sees negative parenting behaviors and wants to criticize or blame. If the foster parent is not present for the visit, she will wonder what is happening and what the child is saying about her, may have safety concerns for the child, will wonder if the visit is going well, and will be mentally and emotionally preparing for the aftermath.

Aftermath

The aftermath of the visit is a critical time for the foster parents as well as for the child. The previous discussion about the child's reactions gives an inkling of what the foster parent will confront after the visit, and much handling of the child's reactions will fall on the foster parent.

If the foster parent does not understand the child's reactions, she will tend to blame the parent, which sends a negative message to the child and interferes with future visits. Even if she understands the reactions, the foster parent experiences a real disruption to the household and resents that (Beyer, 1999a), and she may then give precedence to regaining control of the disruptive behavior over meeting the child's immediate needs for comfort and understanding. If there are other foster children in the home, the foster parent will be concerned about the effects of the child's reactions on these other children (Hess & Proch, 1988). The foster parent may also be confronted with questions regarding the parents and future visits and will struggle with how to provide direct answers (as well as she is able).

The foster parent may also have to deal with reactions from the biological parent, who may express her pain as anger toward the foster parent or criticism of the child's care.

Service Providers

We often forget to consider the effects of visitation on the caseworker and other service providers, but they too are participants in the cycle of events and stages of visitation; and they too affect and are affected by the experiences and reactions of other participants. A central factor for the worker is the sense of responsibility—legal, professional, and ethical. In addition, service providers have specific tasks associated with visitation. (No attempt is made here to sort out the types of service providers that may be involved; the focus in on the primary worker responsible for various aspects of visitation.)

Anticipation

Before the visit, the worker will be busy arranging logistics, which could mean coordinating with all the different participants. But regardless of the care that the worker takes, there will usually be some anxiety about how the visit will come together: Will the transportation arrangements pan out? Will the parent be ready—sober and on time? Will the child or other parties involved be ready? Will adequate preparation have forestalled any avoidable potential problems? In addition, the experienced worker, like the experienced foster parent, anticipates the pain all will experience, knows the visit will be difficult for all, and also understands the positive outcomes that will eventually result from visitation. The worker also always worries about safety issues. Again, despite the best assessment of the situation, the worker is aware that no assessment is 100% foolproof and no visit is 100% predictable. Thus, the worker is concerned about both the child's safety and, understandably, about liability issues if the child is harmed. The worker is torn between providing the most natural and home-like experience for the child and protecting—possibly overprotecting—him.

The Visit

During the visit the worker, like the foster parent, may or may not be present and may be there primarily to observe or to provide on-site intervention. But whatever the case, events can occur that challenge the worker emotionally. For instance, the worker rejoices with the mother and child that they are seeing one another again. At the same time, observing a mother's pain when a child rejects her attentions, a child's pain when the visit is over and separation occurs again, or everyone's pain when a child clings desperately to the mother takes a toll on the worker. The worker shares in everyone's pain and is powerless to prevent it.

At other times the worker's feelings are aroused when behaviors are directed more toward the worker, as when a hurting parent, in the presence of the child, blames the worker for the placement or when a child blames the worker for not letting him go home. In such cases the worker has to handle the situations nondefensively and realistically, focusing on the needs of the child and other participants. Yet, the worker certainly has residual emotions.

Despite the difficulties and without denying them, throughout the visit the worker will retain in his own consciousness and reinforce for all participants the image that change will occur, ensuring that the difficulties never overwhelm the positives.

Aftermath

In the aftermath of the visit the worker, perhaps reeling from everyone's pain, may feel stressed and drained from the sheer emotional impact, helpless to take away others' hurt, angry at verbal abuse from the parent, and anxious about the aftermath for all participants and about what will happen next with the family (Hess,1988). Yet amid these emotions, the worker has serious tasks to accomplish in terms of ensuring that others are helped to deal with the aftermath of the visit, and in terms of accurately recording and accurately interpreting the visit as a basis for ongoing decisionmaking about the child and parent.

Thus, it is important that team members (if the agency uses teams) and especially the worker's *supervisor* support the worker in handling his residual feelings after visitation, helping the worker maintain the strength and assurance to quickly reenter the emotionally charged environment of the next visit.

Others

Earlier we described visitation as an ecological event and established that a variety of participants may be included. It is likely that the first visit will focus on the parent and child, but other visits may include other relatives or friends who are meaningful to the child. The reactions of any participants must be understood and considered to ensure that their involvement adds and does not detract from the furtherance of the work of the parent and child together.

Siblings deserve special mention. It is important to note that relationships between and among siblings may take many forms. Sometimes they may be warm and positive, sometimes negative and upsetting, and frequently ambivalent (Bank & Kahn, 1982). But the bonds between siblings are often strong and deeply intense, regardless of their quality.

Bank and Kahn (1982, p. 19) have noted the following:

> Sibling relationships are an important aspect of the many-colored and many-textured landscape of family life, and children's patterns of behavior and emergence of life scripts occur in the context of these relations as surely as in the context of child—parent relationships. Sibling bonds may be particularly intense when reliable parental care has been lacking. In this situation, siblings will use one another as major influences, or touchstones, in a search for personal identity....Thus, when other relationships cannot be relied upon, intense sibling relationships are activated.

This statement certainly supports the consideration of sibling bonds in relation to child placement and visitation.

Because sibling relationships are so complicated, it is important that the quality, character, and depth of the bond not be assumed or taken for granted in planning to include siblings in visitation. Thus, how other siblings will respond and how the placed child will respond cannot be assumed but must be discovered by careful assessment and well-planned, intelligently observed trials.

Conclusion

Planning, implementing, and maximizing the benefits of visitation may be seen as a complex choreography that involves logistics and, more importantly, relationships. Participants move interactively through time and space, through visitation events and stages, and toward climactic resolution—achievement of the child's permanency plan. In-depth understanding of what participants experience, particularly emotional reactions, during and around visitation is the basis of this elegant choreography and of an artful resolution.

Understanding one's own and others' perspectives and feelings is the basis for empathy, which is the core of all helping behavior. At the beginning of this chapter we referred to development of a complex web of empathy among all parties. This means that the worker is not the only one who must understand feelings and behaviors, that empathy is required not only from the worker but from all participants, and that all participants have mutual helping roles. A generous spirit is required of all, a spirit that is willing to see a wide range of reactions—not only the bright and loving but the dark and hurtful—as for the most part normal human reactions to very difficult and painful situations.

The worker has a special and important role in supporting development of empathy through ongoing insight-focused conversations with participants. But the worker's role goes beyond this. He also uses this understanding to help change behaviors and improve outcomes for participants, particularly the child. Thus, armed with his own deep understanding of the experience of visitation, the worker will do the following:

- *Help participants understand and thus handle appropriately their own reactions to visitation*

   Every participant—parent, child, foster parent, or other—needs to understand what is going on inside herself as she is impelled through this complex process called visitation. This understanding helps each participant gain some sense of control over herself and perhaps over a process, which in many ways is beyond her control. In addition, with this understanding participants are better equipped to modify their reactions and behaviors toward ways that are most apt to lead to successful, productive visitation. For instance, when a mother can consciously associate her tendency to miss visits with her pain, she is in a better position to begin to handle her pain in other ways and to reestablish her regular visits.

- *Help participants understand the reactions of others involved in visitation*

   This understanding will enable them to respond more appropriately to one another rather than responding inappropriately based on misinterpretations of behaviors. Good communication is based on correctly reading the messages and cues of others. Yet during visitation emotions are so high and defensive behaviors so prevalent that messages and cues are distorted. Responding to these distortions can produce downward-spiraling chains of miscommunication. Thus, participants need to be helped to step back and look at the true meaning behind overt behaviors and to form their responses based on these deeper meanings. For instance, when a mother can come to understand that a child's sullenness is not a rejection of her but rather a protection from pain, the mother is more apt to respond with reassurance rather than hurt and anger. Even a child of a certain age can learn that a mother's tardiness is not a sign of rejection but rather an expression of her own pain and discomfort, enabling the child to judge her less harshly.

■ *Manipulate events to assist all participants in working toward better outcomes*

The worker must understand the visitation experience of all participants in order to arrange visitation events for maximal results. As "chief choreographer," the worker encourages the kind of conversations among participants (e.g., "This is hard, and we're all in it together") and behaviors (e.g., flexibility in scheduling of time and place) that support working together and being productive.

■ *Make good decisions regarding permanency goals*

How parents use visitation provides information that the worker uses to determine the most appropriate permanency goal; and if parents do not honor visitation plans or are unable to use visitation productively, a goal may be changed from reunifica tion to some other arrangement. Yet if the parents' struggles around visitation are not properly appreciated, there is danger that their expressions of pain and discom fort—and particularly reactions such as tardiness, missing appointments, self-med icating with substances, or failing to interact appropriately with the child—will automatically be interpreted as disinterest. These behaviors may indeed signal disin terest, but the worker will not know that until he has looked behind the behaviors and provided the opportunity for the parent to develop better insight and thus to modify her visiting behaviors.

■ *Understand expected reactions against which to evaluate excessive or unhealthy reactions*

What has been presented here as expected reactions to visitation covers a wide range of emotions, thoughts, and concerns. Understanding these reactions as something normal allows all participants to observe and handle them routinely and without alarm. But reactions can go beyond what is expected. When, for instance, a child's reactions seem grossly inconsistent with age expectations, the reactions are not amenable to good casework but continue intensely throughout the stages of visitation, or when they are so destructive that productive visitation is not possible, the worker may consider them to be beyond the expected and should consider referral to treatment to supplement the intervention of visitation.

It is important to note here that the focus of this chapter has been on the difficult emotions that emerge during the early phase of visitation and are to some extent relived in each visit. As visitation progresses, if it is skillfully handled, these emotions will become less intense.

We have not extensively addressed the positive emotions associated with visitation. Though early visits are characterized more by pain and ambivalence, again as visitation progresses and is skillfully handled, positive emotions—children's intense excitement in anticipation of a visit, joy at being together, pleasure at learning new skills, happy anticipation of reunification—may become more dominant. Still, the pain and ambivalence may never disappear. The foster parent, while happy about the success of the placement, may experience pain at having to return the child. If the permanency plan is one other than reunification, the parent and child may enter a prolonged (even lifelong) period of dealing with loss. And the worker may rejoice at the achievement of permanency but still worry about the child's future.

For all participants, as they experience the many emotions associated with visitation, the positive motivation to work together comes from the anticipation of a better future—of a child who will achieve a safe and permanent living arrangement in which ongoing development can flourish, and perhaps with a parent who has come through the period of separation stronger and more competent.

Context for
Visitation Services

Visitation, like any other child welfare service, does not occur in isolation but rather occurs within a context that shapes the form that services will assume. Thus, although the primary focus of this publication is direct practice, the discussion would be incomplete without some appreciation of contextual factors that surround visitation and provide the sense of importance, practice guidance, and resources. These factors are very powerful in either supporting or discouraging effective visitation practices.

Therefore, this chapter will begin with a discussion of the Adoption and Safe Families Act of 1997 (ASFA) and its implications for visitation; review CWLA standards in relation to visitation; review the status of state legislation around visitation; look at state agency policy, leadership, and agency resources that support visitation; and discuss supervisory needs in relation to visitation.

ASFA

Federal legislation over the past twenty years has set a context for our thinking regarding visitation, beginning with the passage of Public Law (P.L.) 96–272, the *Adoption Assistance and Child Welfare Act of 1980,* which focused on permanency planning, emphasizing tiered options for achieving permanency—preventing out-of-home placement, reunification, and finally achieving permanency through some other arrangement such as adoption. Though other federal legislation since 1980 has emphasized other aspects of child welfare services (e.g., P.L. 103–66, the *Family Preservation and Family Support Services Program,* which emphasized prevention; and P.L. 103–382, the *Multiethnic Placement Act;* and P.L. 104-188, the *Interethnic Placement Provisions,* which addressed nondiscriminatory practices), it is P.L. 105–89, ASFA, which returns us to broader permanency planning issues. The primary foci and provisions of ASFA have certain implications for visitation, as summarized in Table 1.

Table 1: Summary of ASFA Provisions in Relation to Visitation

ASFA Provision and Focus	Implications for Visitation
Safety is the paramount concern	Visitation should be used both to help parents learn safe parenting practices and to incrementally test their ability to safely parent.
Emphasizes reasonable efforts and identifies circumstances when reasonable efforts are not required	Ensuring that visitation occurs and providing supports for visitation is included in reasonable efforts; lack of support for visitation makes the agency vulnerable in seeking termination of parental rights. The decision to bypass reasonable efforts (including visitation support) requires careful documentation.
Reduced time frames for first permanency hearing (12 months rather than 18 months)	Visitation should begin immediately with the permanency goal clearly the focus.
Begin TPR proceedings for children who have been in care for 15 of the last 22 months (unless the child is with relatives or there is a compelling reason not to TPR, or the family has not received services)	Visitation should begin immediately with the permanency goal clearly the focus; visitation should provide clear evidence that TRP is or is not in the child's best interest; visitation is a most important service that must be provided for the family in terms of reasonable efforts unless it is clearly precluded; use visitation to support TPR and the adoption permanency option.
Concurrent planning option	In response to reduced time frames, concurrent planning (for reunification and some other permanency option) is an important service; visitation is the context in which full disclosure regarding the possibility of various permanency outcomes is exercised and in which testing permanency options occurs.
Emphasis on kinship care	Though a child may be in kinship care, this does not reduce the need for visitation and does not change the purposes of visitation, though there will be special considerations around visitation in relation to kinship care.
Recognition of substance abuse as a significant child welfare issue	Consider special concerns around visitation when substances are involved; consider use of supervised visitation as well as special treatment programs.
Focus on results and accountability; procedural safeguard no longer sufficient	Results include not only safety and permanence but also well-being, suggesting that services, including visitation, must consider the health and development of children in care.
Innovative approaches emphasized	Given the importance of visitation, agencies should be proactive in finding new ways to ensure that it occurs and is effective at meeting its designed purposes.

Thus, although ASFA does not directly address visitation, it is easy to see the importance of visitation and of exemplary visitation practices for supporting the ASFA provisions.

CWLA Standards

Professional standards speak directly to the importance of visitation, and CWLA (1995) has articulated standards that may guide our thinking around visitation. First, CWLA establishes visitation as a right of both children and parents and a parental responsibility.

■ Children in out-of-home placement have the right to "opportunities for continued connection with their family of origin, extended family, and others with whom they have had meaningful relationships, unless contraindicated for reasons of safety" (p. 12).

■ Parents of children in care have the right to "regularly scheduled visits and other contacts with their children unless prohibited by the court for compelling reasons" (p. 13). Likewise, parents have the responsibility to "maintain visiting and other regular contact with the child in care" (p. 14).

CWLA also establishes the child welfare agencies' and foster parents' responsibility to support visitation and defines visitation as including the wider network of kin and friends.

■ Family foster care agencies should support family–child relationships, and "services should be based on a respect for children's ties to their parents, siblings, and kin; and should include visits by and with parents, siblings, and kin unless contraindicated for reasons of safety" (p. 20).

■ "Foster parents, in collaboration with the family foster care agency social worker, should help the children in their care to participate in visits with their parent and have positive experiences during visits and should help them with their feelings about visits before, during, and after the experiences" (p. 48).

■ The agency should help foster parents support the parent–child relationship, including supporting visitation and other contacts (standard 2.40).

■ "Unless indicated to the contrary in the service plan, children should visit with their siblings when they are not placed in the same foster home" (p. 48).

■ "Unless indicated to the contrary in the service plan, visits should be encouraged with the child's kin and friends when these relationships are positive experiences for the child" (pp. 48–49).

CWLA also addresses the purposes and benefits of visitation.

■ "The family foster care agency should recognize parent–child contact as a critical determinant of parent–child reunification and should make use of parental visits to facilitate healthy interactions and attachments between children and their parents and to assess the appropriateness of reunification as a permanency plan" (p. 74). Specific social worker tasks include helping parents understand the purpose of visits, involving the parent and child in writing a visiting plan and giving participants copies, identifying and helping to overcome obstacles to visiting, holding postvisit discussions with all parties as appropriate, and using the visits to assess reunification potential.

■ The agency should support foster parents in their role of supporting visitation and in preparing the child, allowing visits in the foster home whenever possible, and helping the child handle postvisit feelings (standard 2.89).

Besides directly addressing visitation, the CWLA standards also contain language that indicates how agencies should work with families, thus supporting good visitation practices. This includes such things as the responsibility to

■ help children deal with the effects of separation and loss (standards 1.4, 2.37);

■ develop and support service plans (standard 1.7);

■ encourage full participation of children and families in such things as planning activities and team meetings (standard 1.17);

■ involve children, families, and foster parents in assessment and planning (standards 2.20, 2.21, and 2.22); and

■ encourage contacts with parents, kin, and friends through other means (standard 2.45).

Thus, professional standards as articulated through CWLA leave no doubt as to the importance of visitation and provide guidance to agencies around policy and practice.

State Statutes and Court Decisions

Visitation as a permanency planning service receives some support from state statutes and court decisions.

Many states have laws that address visitation. Most are limited but do spell out visitation as a parental right or as a service that the child welfare agency must provide. Others offer more detail, such as spelling out who might be involved in visitation, including siblings and other family or even friends; considering the relationship between the child and parent or other relatives in planning; specifying that the court may require filing of a visitation plan; addressing when visitation may be denied; addressing parental rights for a review hearing if visitation is denied; considering distance and proximity when making placements; and setting time frames for visits (see, for instance, Alaska, Arizona, California, New Hampshire, and New York).

Other state statutes address additional issues. For instance, in some states legislation is the basis for visitation centers that may serve not only families experiencing out-of-home placement due to child maltreatment but also families experiencing divorce (see, for instance, Florida and Connecticut). In addition, the visitation rights of grandparents is an emerging but as yet unresolved issue in relation to both foster care and divorce (see, for instance, Colorado).

The courts also provide some guidance around visitation. For instance, a standing order of the Superior Court for San Francisco Juvenile Division gives specific instructions regarding visitation, stipulating that the first visit should occur within 5 days of placement; that children aged 0 to 5 years should receive at least 6 hours per week of visitation and children aged 6 to 18 years at least three hours per week, but in all cases visits should be as frequent and convenient as possible for all parties; and requirements around missed visits. A Washington, D.C., court ruling (*LaShawn A. versus Dixon Final Modified Order*) states that there must be "a specific schedule of visitation between the child and the child's parent(s) and other appropriate family members, including siblings"; and that

> all visitations between children and their parents and siblings take place in the parent's home unless there are reasons documented in the record that home visits would pose a danger to the child. In all instances, visits shall take place in the most family-like setting possible. The Department shall assure that all children with a permanency goal of return home are permitted to visit with their parent(s) at least once a week, unless the best interest of the child, specifically documented in the child's case record, requires less frequent visitation.

Thus, although state law tends to minimally address visitation, some states and courts have gone further in terms of requiring specific elements.

State Agency Leadership, Policies, and Resources

Although federal legislation, professional standards, and state legislation or court orders may support and encourage visitation and visitation practices, the state child welfare agency is the critical place that good practice will be supported or discouraged. An agency that only adheres to the legal requirements around visitation will fall far short of providing the needed services.

State agency support for visitation begins with the agency director and is manifested in a number of ways, including articulation of a philosophy, policy and practice guidelines, provision of resources, special initiatives, and "counting." Though articulation of a philosophy may appear abstract, in fact it is enormously important. Agency employees, clients, and the general public need to hear from top administration a message that reflects understanding of separation issues and the importance of parent–child ties, respect for family strengths, a presumption of parental desire, ability to rear children safely, and a commitment to provide resources to support families.

Policy and practice guidelines provide the specifics that translate philosophy into good practice. States and agencies will vary in terms of decisions regarding what should appear as policy versus practice guidelines, but both policy and practice guidelines are mechanisms for setting norms that govern practice. The importance of clear policy and practice guidelines has been demonstrated by Proch and Howard (1986). Reviewing case records of 256 randomly selected children in foster care in Illinois, they found a strong connection between plans and actual visitation patterns, indicating the agency's obligation to set the pattern in terms of visitation rather than leaving it to chance. Further, Hess (1988) found that frequency of visits was often beyond the control of the parent and depended on agency policy, practices, and resources. In short, for visitation to occur optimally, practice standards need to be spelled out by the agency. It should not fall to each worker to determine standards.

Elements that should be addressed in either policy or practice guidelines include at least the following (see Hess, 1988; Loar, 1998; County of Erie, 1999; Hess & Proch, 1993; and Hess, 1999, for a discussion of policy and other agency support around visitation):

- The visitation plan should be written and should be part of the overall case plan.

- The visitation plan should address the *full* range of logistics and visitation issues—frequency, time spent, who may visit (e.g., siblings, other family), safety issues, and other appropriate issues.

- The visitation plan should be developed with full parental involvement and child involvement to the extent appropriate.

- The visitation plan should be distributed to all parties involved as appropriate (e.g., parent, child, foster parent, relatives, providers).

- The visitation plan should be regularly reviewed in conjunction with administrative and judicial reviews.

- Decisions around the placement of children in care should consider proximity to parents and siblings so distance is not an obstacle to ongoing contact.

- Support of visitation should be a requirement for foster parents, and the agency should not use foster parents who do not support visitation.

- Guidelines in terms of ensuring child safety during visitation should be provided, and the return home should not be permitted until the family's ability to safely manage extended unsupervised visits has been clearly established.

- The agency should articulate clear prohibitions around withholding visitation for reasons of punishment.

- Expectations of parent(s), foster parents, children (as appropriate), and workers in terms of supporting visitation should be clearly spelled out.

Not only must the agency take a strong position (through philosophy, policy, and practice guidelines) supporting visitation, but also it must allocate resources commensurate with the requirements and expectations. The following resources are needed for full support of visitation:

- Caseloads should be of a size to allow for complete visitation services, including making logistical arrangements, preparing participants for the visit, observing or supervising, conducting postvisit debriefings with various participants, coordinating with other providers or team members, and recording.

- If visitation services or part of visitation services (i.e., observation or supervision) are contracted out, time should be allowed for coordination with providers, because the agency worker maintains responsibility for knowing what has occurred during visits, knowing the parent's progress, and making recommendations regarding permanency.

- Flexible work hours (e.g., extended hours, weekend hours) should be provided (and supported through compensatory time or another mechanism) to ensure that workers can meet family visitation needs.

- Appropriately designed and equipped (e.g., safe, attractive, variety of toys and materials for different ages of children, food preparation area) space for visits should be ensured, through agency visiting rooms, visitation centers, or other controlled environment, to accommodate visitations when the foster home, parent's home, or other locations in the child's natural environment are not appropriate or available.

- Other resources should be available to support visitation. These might include (Hess, 1988; Hess & Proch, 1993; Loar, 1998) provision of transportation through agency staff or volunteers, fares for public transportation, car seats, maps, and petty cash for meals or individual needs.

■ Training should be available to workers, foster parents, and parents around the importance of visitation, agency policy and guidelines, expectations, and how to maximize the benefits of visitation.

■ Supervision should be available to workers to support their decisionmaking around visitation; maximizing the benefits; and handling emotional reactions to visits, including the workers' own reactions as well as those of other participants.

■ Adequate support for foster parents should be available to assist them in carrying out their role of supporting visitation. This might include training, consultation, emotional support, and material support.

The agency may also commit its resources to special initiatives that support state-of-the-art visitation practice. For instance, many agencies now use some form of family group conferencing or mediation to support permanency planning, and these may include visitation planning and monitoring. Others have initiated or contracted out for special visitation initiatives for particular populations, such as families involved in domestic violence or substance use. When the agency is engaged in such special initiatives, it is important that innovations arising from the initiatives be brought into ongoing agency practice.

Last, agency administration shows its support for visitation through its *data collection* and reporting requirements and practices. Workers will attend to whatever is counted and whatever is required for reporting. Most agencies maintain data on such things as child protective services reports, investigations, findings, placements, and moves. What should agencies be counting in terms of visitation? The agency may consider such things as timing of the first visit, frequency of visits, and reviews of visitation plans. In addition, the agency may consider maintaining data on such things as parent satisfaction, obstacles to visitation, association between visitation and reunification, and association between visitation and achievement of permanency, reflecting ASFA's emphasis on not only processes but also outcomes.

Supervision Needs

The supervisor plays a critical role in supporting visitation.

■ As the link between top administration and workers, the supervisor brings agency philosophy, policy, and practice guidelines to the workers, continually supporting the message and ensuring that workers understand it.

■ Supervisors help the workers translate agency philosophy, policy, and practice guidelines into actual practice, developing, implementing, and monitoring visitation plans using the resources available.

■ When resources are inadequate, the supervisor advocates for additional resources.

■ When agency philosophy, policy, and practice guidelines provide inadequate support for state-of-the-art visitation practice, the supervisor, as a child welfare professional, is nonetheless bound by professional standards and promotes professional practice among workers while advocating for advances in philosophy, policy, and practice guidelines.

■ The supervisor assists and supports the worker as she struggles with the many emotions surrounding visitation. Not only must the worker help all participants understand and manage their own feelings and those of other participants, but also she must deal with her own emotions throughout the process, which often reflect the emotions of participants—anger, pain, anxiety, powerlessness (Hess, 1988).

■ The supervisor supports the worker's decisionmaking regarding permanency based on the visitation experience.

■ The supervisor can communicate what is important by maintaining data on specific aspects of visitation (e.g., parent satisfaction) despite its not being required by the agency. In fact, judicious data keeping can be very supportive of good practice and of staff as it can recognize and reward behaviors and outcomes that workers instinctively know are important but are not usually recognized.

Summary

This chapter has looked at visitation contextually, in terms of ASFA; professional standards; state legislation and court orders; agency policy, practice, and resources; and supervision. We cannot over-emphasize the importance of these contextual factors in ensuring that the high quality of practice we know is needed becomes a reality.

All agencies are strapped for resources, and decisions always must be made about fair and equitable allocation of resources. Too often workers are left to bear the burden of the imbalance between requirements and resources. Yet agencies can do much to support good visitation practice, despite resource limitations, through communication of a set of beliefs about visitation that recognize its centrality as a permanency planning service.

Variations and Issues in Visitation

Chapter 4 described a holistic, integrated view of visitation with complex reciprocal interactions among various parties throughout each visitation event and through the entire process and all stages of visitation. We have also seen that visitation is planned, carefully choreographed, and purposefully directed toward achievement of a particular case goal. In addition, the character of visitation evolves, changing throughout the stages.

Thus, planning around visitation is not a one-time event but rather an *ongoing process,* as the worker responds to the demands of each stage as well as to new knowledge about the family that is learned as they carry out the plan. In planning and constantly adapting visitation, there are several dimensions along which decisions must be made, so that each visitation plan is clearly suited to the family and the situation. Because these dimensions are interrelated, no one can be discussed entirely discretely from all others. Yet, we have somewhat artificially separated them to allow focus on each one in this chapter. The chapter will present several overriding issues that influence other decisions around visitation, explore five dimensions of visitation planning, and discuss additional special issues.

It is important to note that there is no one way to plan visitation; rather, it must be individualized. In a recent state survey, staff and parents agreed that every case is different and needs to be handled accordingly (Clemons 1999).

Overriding Issues

Certain issues or factors are particularly important in their power to drive all other decisions about visitation. These include safety issues, the permanency goal, time in care, familial and cultural variables, age of the child, and the agency's ability to handle logistics.

Safety Issues

Safety issues loom large in all child welfare work, because most children who come into care do so as a result of some form of maltreatment. But safety takes on special importance in relation to visitation. In this situation the child is in the custody of the agency; and the agency is responsible for ensuring that its own "treatment," including visitation, not only protects the child from the initial threat of harm but also does not reendanger the child through exposing him to new threats. When parents have been violent toward children, substance involvement makes parental behavior unpredictable, the parent's neighborhood is dangerous, or sexual abuse is involved, workers are particularly concerned that visitation not expose the child to unnecessary risk. This concern will influence all aspects of visitation planning. (The agency may have developed its own risk assessment or safety assessment protocol. If not, such instruments are available and may be useful to support the worker's clinical judgement.)

The dilemma for the work is, of course, to balance realistic and necessary caution against the parties' rights for visitation and, more importantly, the benefits of visitation. Solutions are to be found only in creative planning, making decisions that preserve both benefits and safety. Openness with participants about the dilemma—the agency's responsibility to protect as well as its sincere desire to support visitation—can greatly increase the creative options.

Permanency Goal

Because visitation is a service designed to further or to help determine the permanency goal, the permanency goal may be seen as an important overriding variable that shapes visitation. Thus, if it is clear that reunification is the goal, elements of the visitation plan—timing of events, content, and other factors—will be determined with that goal in mind. On the other hand, if another option is the choice, decisions may be different (e.g., termination of parental rights [TPR] and adoption may suggest a gradual decrease in visits and an emphasis on grief work more than parenting skills).

The advent of concurrent planning has added a new twist to visitation. Some agencies were practicing concurrent planning before the enactment of the Adoption and Safe Families Act (ASFA), but the legislation emphasized that practice as an option. In concurrent planning, the agency and participants are considering more than one permanency goal at the same time, perhaps reunification and adoption, and using visitation diagnostically to help parties discover the best option for the child. This allows the family and agency to make an honest effort toward reunification, even if it is not the most likely option, without losing precious time in moving toward TPR and adoption or some other option. Thus, in using concurrent planning, the agency gives the parent the best chance to rehabilitate (or habilitate) but at the same time explores other options to ensure that movement toward the best possible permanent plan proceeds as quickly as possible. In concurrent planning, visitation elements would probably include such things as numerous opportunities for a parent to demonstrate ability to care for the child, intensive services (within visitation itself or adjunct services) to demonstrate reasonable efforts, and careful observation and documentation of parent–child interactions.

Later discussion will present more details on visitation in relation to other options—long-term foster care, adoption, or kinship care of various sorts.

Stages and Time in Care

Time in care will influence visitation planning, and the plan that is optimal for early visitation will be obsolete in later phases. Clearly, the requirements for visitation change *from* early, to middle, to late stages in care. For instance, during early stages visits are apt to be court set or determined by agency norms. The focus will be on establishing visitation patterns early, easing the immediate pain of separation, and ensuring the proper level of safety precaution. But as the case progresses and participants get to know one another better, visits will be changed to reflect such things as the tasks that must be accomplished and the characteristics and needs of the particular family. Later, as the time of reunification or another permanency plan nears, the frequency, place, restrictions, and content of visits will change toward preparation for the transition (Hess, 1988).

Idiosyncratic Family and Cultural Variables

Each family is different, so each visitation plan should be different. Although early plans may be somewhat stereotypical, as the participants get to know one another better, the plan should begin to reflect the characteristics of the family. For instance, each family will have a different set of significant relatives and friends who might be included in the visitation; the places and organizations to which the family and child are attached will be different; and emotional reactions to visits and thus parental ability to comply with the plan and needed assistance will differ. It is important that these differences be allowed to emerge and that family uniqueness be noticed, honored, and reflected in visitation planning.

Cultural differences may also affect planning. Family interactional patterns, division of responsibilities, sense of community responsibility for children, ways of dealing with authority, and parenting style preferences are all culturally influenced. Always learn about and respect these differences and discuss them with families.

Age of Child

The age of the child in care influences the visitation plan. For instance, infants and very young children are so vulnerable to separation trauma and so bereft of coping strategies that they need more frequent visits than older children and adolescents might need. Scheduling of visits is more of an issue with older children and adolescents who are engaged in structured activities outside the home. They can feel, and rightly so, resentful when visitation plans are made for them, conflicting with their other activities and without their knowledge or consent. (Considering these other activities is important not only as a show of respect, but also because maintaining normalcy outside the home is an important coping strategy for older children and adolescents.) The content of visits is certainly age-related, as the activities enjoyed and the level of cognitive understanding vary according to age. The place may also be a factor, as older children and adolescents have more connections to people, places, and organizations in the community than do younger children.

Agency's Ability to Handle Logistics

An agency's or worker's ability to handle the logistics of visitation will greatly influence all other variables. And if an agency is expected to respond to the needs of families, it is important that the agency provide the resources (e.g., policy, training, time, dollars) to support a wide range of visitation arrangements. This subject has been thoroughly discussed in chapter 5, but it is mentioned here because it is such an important factor in influencing visitation.

Dimensions of Visitation Planning

There are several important dimensions around which decisions must be made in visitation planning. These include timing of the visits, where the visits will take place, who will participate, content of the visits, and what special controls might need to be in place to assure child safety. Of course, each of these interrelated decisions will be influenced by the issues previously discussed.

Timing of Visits

Decisions that must be made regarding the timing of visits include how soon after placement the first visit should occur, how often visitation should occur subsequently, and the duration of each visit.

Hess and Proch (1993) recommend that the first visit occur within the first 48 hours and that visits occur at least weekly after that. Chiancone (1997) relates frequency and duration of visits to the age of the child, noting that for younger children visits should be more frequent and briefer; infants and toddlers need several visits a week to foster attachment.

Frequency and duration of visits also relates to safety issues, agency resources, and the stage in the visitation process. When safety issues are a major concern and visits have to be closely monitored, both frequency and duration could be affected by the difficulties in providing appropriate supervision. In terms of stages, it is generally believed that, as a parent has demonstrated that she can safely care for the child and the time for reunification is approaching, there should be a gradual increase in the duration of visits, moving from one hour or several hours during the day toward overnights and weekends. This graduation, this careful and gentle moving of the child back into the home rather than abruptly reuniting him with the family, gives parties the opportunity to experience the reunification in small doses and recognize and confront any potential difficulties so they will not lead to disruption of the reunification. It also gives the parent the opportunity to carefully try out new parenting skills and make small corrections before the final reunification.

Chiancone (1997) notes that consistency is key; whatever schedule is decided on, it should be regular, predictable, and easy for all parties to adhere to, because missed visits are very difficult to handle emotionally and destructive of efforts toward building or maintaining attachment. In addition, the schedule should be reviewed regularly to ensure that it changes as the needs of the family change.

Place of Visits

Many options are available for where visits might take place. Each has its advantages, and the choice of place should be purposeful. In addition, there is no reason that the same place should be used all the time. Although providing some consistency and regularity is important for the child, there are times that a change is useful.

Child's Home

Hess & Proch (1993) state that the preferred setting for visits is the child's home, unless this is precluded for safety reasons. The home has certain advantages. First, it is familiar to the child and can satisfy his longing for what was left behind. The child returns to his own room, toys, and environs. Yet, during the first few visits at home, it may be particularly difficult for the child to understand that she has to leave again and return to the foster home. Another advantage is that it puts the parent and child back in their natural setting for practice and demonstration of parenting skills. Because it is in the home that reunification will eventually occur (if that is the plan and all goes well), it is there that the parent must learn to provide adequate care for the child.

If there is concern that visits in the home will be dangerous for the child, it is not an option. The danger could emanate from specific parental behaviors (e.g., the parent's drinking in the home) or from environmental sources (e.g., known substance users in and out of the home). In such cases, another location should be selected until such time that safety is no longer a question. Of course, the closer the time for reunification, the more important that visits be in the child's own home. If during the final phases of work with a family safety at home is still an issue, the permanency goal may need to be reexamined or, in the case of concurrent planning, a goal other than reunification given priority. On the other hand, the worker may help the parent find a safer home and safer neighborhood so reunification can occur.

Foster Home

Another option for location of visits is the foster home. For this option to be offered, it must be clearly accepted by both staff and foster parents. A recent county survey revealed that, although staff believed visits in foster homes were appropriate, a majority of foster parents did not (County of Erie Department of Human Services, Office of Children and Youth study 1999). Thus, the success of this option will depend heavily on how the agency has defined the foster parent role, including whether policy or practice standards stipulate that foster parents must agree to visits in their home. Visiting in the foster home is consistent with foster parents' seeing themselves as role models and teachers, and being willing to form a relationship with the biological parent that is supportive of improving parenting skills and of eventual reunification. In reality, some foster parents will be open to hosting visits. Others may not; but with experience, training, and support, they may later change their minds and welcome birth parents into their home.

Agency Visiting Room

Sometimes a neutral setting such as an agency visiting room may be the place of choice, if such a room is provided within the child welfare agency or a cooperating agency. If there are known safety issues or if safety has not been clearly established, the agency visiting room adds an element of protection and control. Sometimes the agency visiting room may be used for special teaching purposes. A well-equipped room offers a variety of opportunities for guiding parents in playing appropriately with their children or performing various caregiving activities (e.g., cooking, bathing and changing an infant). If the room has a one-way mirror, observers can be there unobtrusively and provide their comments either immediately or later. Video equipment may also be available, allowing very specific postvisit analysis.

Visitation Center

When there are significant safety concerns and visits must be closely monitored, an increasingly available option is a visitation center. Visitation centers (discussed in more depth later in this publication) are specifically created and staffed to offer supervised visits and may also include a range of support services. They have been used primarily to manage visits amid contentious divorces (which might include severe conflict around custody and even danger of abduction) or other highly dangerous situations (e.g., spouse abuse, drug involvement). Having a safe, secure, neutral place such as this for visits can make the difference between continuing visits and terminating them altogether (Tortorella 1996), an option to be avoided except in extreme situations.

Child's Natural Environment

A range of sites from the child's natural environment may be chosen, places that are both meaningful to the child and appropriate for meeting the goals of visitation. The home of another relative may be an option if the child has spent time there and it is deemed safe. A fast-food restaurant that the child likes could also be an alternative visitation site. Also, the parent could accompany the child to an activity the child enjoys, such as a ball game or school play. Even taking the child along during everyday activities such as grocery shopping or a trip to the neighborhood laundry provides connection to familiar people, places, and things that can reassure the child and support the child's "elaborate package of belonging" (Millham et al. 1986: p. 102).

Professional Appointments

The parent may accompany the child to professional appointments (e.g., medical appointments, school meetings, therapy sessions). This reinforces, for both child and parent, the parent's continuing involvement in and responsibility for the child's well-being and also helps keep the parent abreast of the child's developmental progress.

Who Will Participate?

Though our discussion thus far has focused on visitation between a parent, usually the mother, and her child, in reality visitation can involve many combinations of participants. Although there are no simple answers as to who should be involved, helpful questions to ask in making this decision might include the following:

■ Who do the parent and child suggest should be involved?

■ What part (if any) did the person play in the maltreatment (particularly where sexual or severe physical abuse is involved), and can the child be adequately protected?

- What positive role did the person play in the child's life?

- What positive role might the person play in the child's current and future life?

- Overall, how can visitation with this person contribute toward achievement of the permanency goal?

- Does the child for any reason veto visits that include this person?

Fathers

Fathers are often forgotten or underused in visitation planning (Millham et al., 1986). Though they are in the minority, still many children in care come from two-parent families; and both the mother and father may be involved in visitation with the child, either together or separately. The mother and father may be married and living together; the father figure may actually be a stepfather; the mother and father may be divorced and living apart; or the father, whether living with or apart from the mother, may have never been married to her. If the father plays a significant parenting role, it is essential that he be involved, because the eventual permanency option must in that case consider the ability of the parental pair to keep the child safe. In any case, the role and potential contribution of the father should be explored with the family.

Siblings

Siblings should always be considered in visitation planning. Sibling visitation can be complex, because of the variety of arrangements in which they might be living. For instance, all the child's siblings may still be living at home; they may be living with other relatives; they may be placed in the same foster home as the child; they may be placed in several different foster homes; or they may be living in any combination of these arrangements. Though the scattering of siblings is not desirable, it can occur. It may even be planned, if there is a good reason why the siblings should not be placed together (e.g., abusive sibling relationships). Thus, arranging for sibling visits can be a logistical nightmare. But considering the importance of sibling bonding (discussed in Chapter 4), it should always be considered and ruled out only if there are clear reasons (e.g., related to child safety and well-being, a parent's inability to handle more than one child at a particular point, a child's need for individual attention at a certain point). Logistical issues, though difficult, should be addressed using the creativity and assistance of all participants.

Pets

For some children, their closest "siblings" are actually pets. Though to some it may seem strange to discuss pets in this context, those who have had pets may remember that pets can be our most trusted confidants, faithful companions, and greatest source of support. So do not neglect to inquire about pets during visitation planning.

Other Relatives

Other relatives should also be considered. It is important to remember that the degree of the relationship is not as important as the significance of the relative to the family and child. The role of other relatives may range from simply being a supportive presence that keeps the child connected to his preplacement landscape to providing supervision or helping to teach the parent new skills. On the other hand, the relative could actually be the child's current or future caregiver (e.g., kinship care, guardianship, relative adoption).

Grandparents

Particular attention has been given recently to the legal rights of grandparents in relation to visiting their grandchildren, and the issue has become quite controversial and continues to evolve. Looking primarily at instances of family dissolution, states (driven by high divorce rates, family mobility, and political activism of older citizens) are increasingly recognizing the value of intergenerational nurturance (Hartfield, 1996). Yet, this is balanced against a parent's right to privacy and protection from outside interference unless lack of contact is causing the child demonstrable harm (Cestero, 1997). Whatever decisions are made concerning grandparent visitation in situations of divorce will certainly also influence thought and legal decisions regarding children in placement. Meanwhile, for child welfare the decision to include grandparents should be driven by the same factors as those guiding decisions regarding inclusion of other participants (in the absence of state law to the contrary).

Friends

Friends are often as important to the family as relatives and may even be considered "fictive kin." Thus, they too should be considered in visitation planning.

Professionals and Other Helpers

Professionals and other helpers may also be included. Primary among these are foster parents, as the visits might even be in their home. Agency policy or practice guides may even stipulate that they should participate. They have a valuable role in terms of building a helpful relationship with the parent, informally modeling effective parenting behaviors, and formally observing or supervising visits on a frequent basis.

How other professionals are involved can vary greatly. For instance, some agencies may use specially trained visitation observers or supervisors who are either volunteers or paid professionals and are considered part of a visitation team. At other times, a family may agree for a child or parent's therapist to observe, affording an opportunity for the therapist to see firsthand the client's progress.

Content of Visits

Though this issue is at the heart of visitation planning, the question of content of visits—what will happen during the parent and child's time together—is too often neglected or inadequately addressed. Beyer (1999a) has noted that visits tend to be perfuntory, with little attempt to use them to change parenting behaviors. This is unfortunate, because content will largely determine how productive visitation is. Yet, a central dilemma around visitation is the need for participants to be "natural" around one another while engaging in purposeful activities, often under the scrutiny of others.

We know that visitation is, under the best of circumstances, an unnatural situation, as the parent and child who are accustomed to having free and unfettered access to one another must shift to periods of brief, preplanned time together. Add to that the enormous emotions aroused around visits, and nothing about it feels natural. Yet this is the atmosphere in which we require the parent to learn, improve, and demonstrate ability to safely parent a child.

The resolution to this dilemma will be at best a compromise. Nonetheless, the worker, drawing on the expertise and resources of all participants, can manipulate the content to best advantage by discovering the activities and habits of interaction that are most usual for the family and then discovering how to use or modify these to accomplish the visitation purposes. For instance, if the parent and child like to cook together, these occasions can be used to improve the parent's ability to give directions to the child (e.g., age appropriate, tone of voice), ability to correct (e.g., supporting the child's intent while offering new information about the actual execution of a task), and ability to pick up on cues (e.g., know when the child is tired of the activity). Besides addressing parenting and child development issues, visitation content will also focus on such things as supporting parent-child attachment and ongoing permanency planning.

Controls

Visitation is so important that even when significant safety issues are present, the worker should make maximal efforts to preserve visitation. Only in limited situations should visitation be denied. Faller (1993) has suggested that visits be denied when there is danger of abuse even under supervision, visitation would be traumatic to the child, or the child strongly objects to the visit. Chiancone (1997) has suggested a temporary restriction on visits of a child with the alleged abuser until after a child appears in court, if he is to do so. This might be necessary both to avoid tainting the testimony and in recognition of the child's vulnerable position at this point in the proceedings. In addition, if sexual abuse is involved, the court may believe it necessary to restrict visits until certain conditions are met (Schafran et al., 1996).

Thus, because of the importance of visitation even when child safety has not been clearly established, agencies need to use a variety of controls to address the safety issues so the parent–child contact can occur or continue. These are frequently used when two parents are involved and their relationship is contentious or abusive, in cases of sexual abuse, and when alcohol and other drugs are a significant factor.

Controls most frequently combine a (1) a secure place, (2) observation and supervision, and (3) agreements specifying conditions of visitation. As already discussed, the secure place may be an agency visiting room or a visitation center. In addition, for lower levels of risk, the foster parent's home or public places such as malls may be considered secure, because neither would allow the parent and child to be alone together unobserved. Observation or supervision may be provided by the worker, the foster parent, a volunteer or professional observer, or another person that all participants agree on. Especially in volatile situations, though, it is important that the observer be well trained and prepared to handle crises; and it is best if that observer is not a foster parent or a family member.

Rules around visitation may be formalized in agreements between the parent and other parties. Hewitt (1991) describes a model of therapeutic visitation in which a therapist meets separately with the child, alleged abuser, and other parent and compiles a list of appropriate behaviors that meets the child's approval and that the alleged abuser promises to follow. In addition, the alleged abuser tells the child that it is all right to report any inappropriate touching.

Whatever levels and types of controls are used, it is important to remember that not only must the worker and other adult participants feel comfortable with the arrangements, but also the child must feel safe and secure (Chiancone, 1997).

Special Issues

Three special issues that will influence visitation are type of care, incarceration, and ethical concerns.

Type of Care

So far, we have discussed visitation primarily in terms of a child's being in care with foster parents who are not related. But children are often in other types of care. Visitation is also an important service when children are in kinship foster care (an increasingly popular option), group care, and even adoptive homes.

Kinship Foster Care

Kinship care is the full-time nurturing and protection of children by relatives, members of their tribes or clans, godparents, stepparents, or other adults who have a kinship bond with the child (CWLA, 2000). It is the fastest growing out-of-home care arrangement, and this growth is likely to continue for some time (Courtney, 1996). Historically, provision of care for children by kin has always been an important informal service, particularly within the African American community (Courtney, 1996; Gleeson et al., 1997). But it has only recently become a significant service of the child welfare system. Reasons cited for its popularity are the emphasis of federal legislation (first P.L. 96–272 and more recently ASFA) on family-like care; increasing numbers of children entering care, coupled with decreasing nonrelative foster care providers; and clarification of the legality of making foster care payments to relatives.

Kinship care has many strengths, including that it respects a child's family and cultural heritage (Mills & Usher, 1996); kinship care placements are less likely to disrupt than nonrelative placements (Gleeson et al., 1997); and children reunified after kinship care placements are less apt to reenter care than are children reunified after nonrelative placements (Gleeson et al., 1997).

Yet, issues have been raised concerning kinship care. It appears that kin are less apt to adopt than are nonrelative foster parents (Gleeson et al., 1997). In addition, the meaning of permanency has been questioned (e.g., is long-term placement with a relative in itself permanency?), though most professionals still view reunification, adoption, or guardianship as the most desirable permanency options. Thus, permanency planning is the central issue in kinship care as in other out-of-home care arrangements.

How is visitation affected by the foster caregiver's being kin? This has not been empirically examined, but we do know some questions that need to be answered as we think about visitation as a service for kinship foster care (Jackson, 1996).

■ **What is the kin's ability to protect the child?**

Research suggests that children in kinship care are not at higher risk for abuse and neglect than children in foster care (Benedict, et al. 1996). Kinship caregivers are generally quite able to protect the child. In fact, in many instances, protection of the child is the caregiver's primary reason for stepping forward to provide care. In some instances, however, particularly if there is a long history of the parent's being in the home of the kinship caregiver, the family may find it difficult to set limits in terms of the parent's access to the child. In these instances, the family often can be assisted in structuring for child safety.

■ *Is there ongoing conflict between the parent and caregiver?*

Relations between the parent and kin may be excellent. But if conflict exists, it is important that the child not be brought into the conflict during visits.

■ *Does multigenerational child maltreatment exist?*

One of the early fears regarding kinship care was that, assuming that child maltreatment was intergenerationally transmitted, placing a child in the care of a relative would be subjecting him to the same danger that existed in the home of his parent. This is as yet undocumented, and research has shown that the abusive or neglectful parent is often the only dysfunctional member of the family (Meyer & Link, 1990). Research also suggests that kinship caregivers have more positive and nurturing attitudes toward the children in their care than foster parents (Berrick, Barth, and Needell, 1994; Gebel, 1996). Current thinking emphasizes that the relative such as a grandparent has matured, may have less stress in her life, or may have herself received some sort of intervention that would enable her to provide an excellent home for the child. A thorough assessment should explore the caregiver's ability and willingness to provide safe and nurturing care to the child, informing decisions regarding child safety and visitation.

■ *How well can the kinship caregiver carry out the parenting role?*

Can the relative teach and model parenting skills, focus appropriately on permanency planning, and use the full services available through the agency to promote the child's well-being?

■ *How will the triad of child, parent, and relative (as opposed to nonrelative) caregiver work?*

Supervising kinship care, while containing elements of nonrelative foster care supervision, involves intensive family work. Prior to, during, and following visits, the worker will need to help the family to recognize and address family rituals, secrets, patterns, loyalties, and ghosts. The family's previously existing relationships will both strengthen and complicate the work that needs to be done to achieve safety and permanency for the child.

■ *Will it be difficult for the family to adjust to a formal visitation plan if they are used to informal interaction?*

A history of easy, ongoing contact can be another important strength of kinship care. Yet, if family is used to a high level of informal interaction, the structure imposed by a formal care arrangement may seem strange and unnecessary. Still, a formal visitation plan needs to be negotiated and implemented. Though the worker should respect the uniqueness of the family's historical patterns of interaction, the agency's responsibility for ensuring child safety, timely permanency, and well-being must not be compromised.

■ *How do all participants view permanency?*

Research suggests that the majority of kin are willing to care for the child until the child becomes independent through custody, guardianship, or adoption of the child (Link, 1996; McLean & Thomas, 1996). Workers need to determine early on if the kinship caregivers see their care as a permanent arrangement for the child and whether they can support efforts toward reunification. Kinship caregivers also should be pro vided with clear information about permanency options, including reunification, guardianship and adoption, and helped to discuss what would be best for the child, themselves, and the birth parents.

■ *How will extended family be involved?*

Jackson (1996) found that workers tended not to involve extended family in planning for a child in kinship care. Yet, wide family involvement may be necessary for supporting the kinship caregiver (e.g., providing transportation to appointments, providing respite care for the provider, enforcing family boundaries). Thus, extended family members should be included as appropriate in visitation as well as coplanning around permanency.

■ *If reunification is the plan, what will be the future relationship between the child, parent, and caregiver?*

Sometimes a nonrelative foster parent will continue to have a role in the child's life after reunification, but in the case of kinship caregivers, this will almost surely be the case. Thus, the final stage of visitation will have to address what that ongoing role will be so that this is clear and acceptable to all parties.

■ *If the plan is for TPR and adoption, what desires and issues might the kin have around adoption?*

And what information might they need to make an informed decision? If a child has had a successful experience in kinship care and reunification is not an option, it may be desirable for the relative to adopt the child, providing familial and cultural continuity and negating the need for moving the child to a new placement. Issues must be realisti-cally addressed (e.g., fears of disloyalty, financial considerations, and contingency plans for the care of the child in the case of older caregivers) and the decision handled openly among participants, including the child, during visitation and other family sessions.

■ ***Is guardianship a reasonable option? And what information might kin need to make an informed decision about guardianship?***

If the kinship caregivers are not comfortable with adoption, guardianship is often a desirable option, particularly if the state is able to fund such an arrangement. Again, this decision should be handled openly among participants, including the child, during visitation and other family sessions.

Group Care

In the past, families were often neglected when children were in group care. But recently the philosophy of family-centered practice has greatly influenced practices. Today, group care facilities recognize not only the importance of family involvement but also their unique resources for supporting visitation. Group care facilities often have very good space available for visits. And they often have a staff accustomed to working flexible hours who can provide supervision and observation and can meet with groups of families at a visitation. Some group care facilities have converted space to enable families to stay overnight at the facility, allowing for increased visitation between children and their parents.

Adoption

Traditionally, adoption has been considered a confidential transaction, the birth parents having no knowledge of the adoptive parents and the child and adoptive parents having no knowledge of the birth parents. If this were still the case, visitation would not be an issue. But, as adoptees and birth parents began to talk more openly about their loss and lifelong grief; as adoptees began to express curiosity about their genetic histories, particularly in light of new findings regarding the role of genetics in a range of illnesses; and as the stigma attached to unmarried childbearing has lessened, adoptions have moved toward greater openness (Melina & Roszia, 1993).

Open adoption can take an infinite variety of forms, including all types and levels of contact between the biological parent and child. It is not the purpose here to evaluate open adoption but rather to recognize that it will likely involve some form of visitation. And, if this is a child welfare case, the child welfare worker (before finalization or as part of postadopt services) may be involved in helping the participants frame and implement an open adoption agreement that includes a visitation plan. Unlike visitation plans in foster care, this will not be a binding agreement but rather a statement of intent that reflects the best interests of the child. The agreement should include many of the same things as a visitation agreement for foster care visitation: the types of communication that will be acceptable (e.g., letters, calls, visits), frequency of contacts, any supervision needs or other restrictions, involvement of siblings and extended family, and logistics (Melina & Roszia, 1993).

Visitation of extended family (particularly grandparents) with children who have been adopted is particularly controversial, with neither the law nor the child welfare field clear about the issue. Though legally grandparents have no visitation rights in nonrelative adoptions, there may be a moral obligation involved. Most courts still uphold the sanctity of family privacy, but some judges are allowing visitation. This is a quickly changing field, and for the time being workers should be aware of any pertinent state statutes and judicial decisions, while keeping the best interest of the child in the forefront (Oppenheim & Bussiere, 1996).

As with foster care visitation, there are tasks to be accomplished, but they are different. Rather than being driven by time-limited permanency planning, the visitation is about forging lifelong relationships. Rather than teaching the skills of custodial parenting, it teaches the skills for a lifelong supportive role that is different from custodial parenting. Early in the adoption emotions arise from the adoptive family's claiming the child, the child's attaching to the family, and the child and biological parent's dealing with loss. It is to be expected that the needs and emotions of participants will change over the months and years, so any agreement must include provision for renegotiation.

Most adoptions of children in foster care are by their foster parents. Thus, although visitation may have begun with reunification as the permanency goal, at some point that goal changed. This shift significantly affects visitation, as participants' relationships and tasks will have to change to achieve the new goal. For foster parents it means moving from teaching the parent to receive the child back into her home to instead focusing on the child remaining with the foster parent and what that might imply.

Incarceration

When men are incarcerated, it is likely that the mother of their children continues with their care. But increasingly women are being incarcerated, and their children are most apt to be in care with someone other than their father. The most frequent care arrangement for children is with a relative (CWLA, 1998). Usually, the arrangement will be informal, and the child's grandmother or another relative will provide the needed care without the involvement of child welfare. But if a child is already in care, the parent cannot arrange care. Or if an informal arrangement breaks down, child welfare services are likely to come into play and a formal kinship foster care arrangement or a nonrelative foster care arrangement is established.

The fact of a parent's incarceration in no way obviates the need for or the parent's and child's right to the full range of child welfare services, including visitation. In fact, it has been estimated that approximately one-half of incarcerated parents receive no visits from children, and others receive only infrequent visits (CWLA, 1998; Seymour, 199, p. 473; Snell, 1994). Clearly there are such formidable obstacles to visitation that, despite its documented importance, it is often neglected. These include the following, as described by Wright (2000):

Distance—Although good practice dictates that out-of-home placements be near the parent(s) to facilitate visitation, the incarceration of a parent usually means considerable distance, since prisons are located centrally to serve a large geographical area. In addition, because there are fewer women prisoners than men, women's prisons are apt to be fewer in number and so more apt to be farther away from children. This makes visits more difficult. Families may have to dedicate a whole day to travel the distance, making visits less frequent than if the distance were less. In addition, for many families the cost of travel to the prison is an issue. For workers, pressed with other duties, sacrificing a whole day primarily for travel may be a de-motivator.

Hours and scheduling—The hours during which visits are allowed may pose problems. If they are only within the hours of the work day, caregivers may have trouble participating; if they are outside regular work hours, the worker may have difficulty visiting. In addition, scheduling procedures may be cumbersome or poorly understood, resulting in delays. Arranging for visiting where siblings are involved presents other challenges both due to getting children from possibly different homes to the prison and the possible lack of a place at the prison in which several children can be managed.

Accommodations—Even approaching a prison may be intimidating, given some prison's visible security mechanisms, such as wire fencing and guard towers. Generally, the atmosphere is inhospitable to children. There are usually no separate waiting rooms for children, and visits might be in cubicles that lack privacy, adding to the difficulty of expressing real emotions, either positive or negative, or discussing important personal issues (CWLA, 1998; Seymour, 1998, pp. 473, 481; Bloom, 1995; Women's Prison Association, 1996). Sometimes visits occur through glass barriers. In addition, facilities may be dirty, noisy, and overheated (CWLA ,1998; Hairston, 1998, p. 625).

Procedures and requirements—Prisons will have procedures and requirements, often connected with security, that are uncomfortable or humiliating. There may be a prolonged process of clearing for visits that last less than one-half hour. There may be pat and frisk searches and rude treatment (CWLA, 1998; Hairston, 1998, p. 625), since inside the prison outsiders may be seen as unwelcome guests or intruders, and contact between outsiders and prisoners poses serious threat to security (CWLA, 1998;

Hairston, 1998, p. 625; Katz, 1998, p. 504). Security precautions geared to the occasional inmate who will try to sneak contraband in, possibly even in a child's diaper, may appear totally unreasonable and offensive to children, foster caregivers, and workers who are there only to support the parent-child relationship.

Appearance and behavior of parent—Sometimes the appearance and behavior of the parent may seem strange and frightening to the child, particularly during the first visit. The parent may be in prison garb or other clothing the child doesn't recognize. She may not have the same hairdo or makeup, either because of not having access to the same beauty aides or lack of motivation. In addition, behavior may be different because of her shame over the crime and incarceration, discomfort with seeing the child in that setting, or discomfort with the poor accommodations for the visit. Both the different appearance and behavior introduce a strangeness into the situation that creates distance in the parent-child relationship.

Jails—Jails pose special obstacles to visitation. Although they are generally closer to the incarcerated woman's home than are prisons and thus more accessible to family, they may be less child-friendly. Unlike prisons, jails almost universally require noncontact visits, with communication restricted to use of a phone through glass or mesh (CWLA 1998; Katz, 1998, p. 504; Henrique, 1982).

Emotional components—All these factors contribute to a flood of complex emotions poorly understood by the parent, child, caregiver, and perhaps worker. As a result, sometimes parents don't want children to visit and children themselves are tentative about the visit, while caregivers and worker may point to the unpleasant emotions as a reason to postpone or discontinue visits (CWLA, 1998; Beckerman, 1998, p. 517; Hairston, 1998).

While visitation is the primary and preferred means for maintaining contact and positive relationships between incarcerated parents and their children, because of the difficulties with visitation it is good to supplement visits with other forms of communication, such as telephone calls and letters, as might be done for other families. But there are also obstacles associated with these forms of communication. For instance, prisoners do not have free and unfettered access to telephones. Though letters can be a good option, depending on the literacy levels (CWLA, 1998; Seymour, 1998, p. 473; Snell, 1994), outgoing letters may have been stamped with warnings that they are from a correctional facility, and the child or caregiver may find this offensive (CWLA 1998; Hairston, 1998, p. 627). Each family might also add its other ways to support the relationship. For instance, the mother may tape-record messages or readings from a child's favorite books, or the caregivers might send pictures of the child enjoying everyday activities. Whatever forms of communication can be found (and are allowed) to maintain and support a positive parent-child relationship, to keep the reality of one another alive, will further permanency planning and reduce trauma to the child.

Agencies need to have mechanisms for ensuring that they are working effectively with this population, which might include special training for all staff, specially trained workers or units, policies that address incarceration, and agreements between the child welfare agency and corrections.

Ethical Concerns

Several ethical concerns arise in relation to visitation. These center around confidentiality, full disclosure, and reasonable efforts.

Confidentiality

Confidentiality becomes a particularly difficult issue as we expand the number of people involved with a family. We have described an expanded view of visitation that goes beyond the parent and child. We have suggested that a variety of relatives, friends, and professionals might be involved in visits. Yet as the pool of participants is expanded, what assurance does the family have that its business will remain its business; and that personal details of their lives will not become known and discussed among family, friends, neighbors, and other professionals more widely than they would desire? Though there is no simple solution, following are some guidelines:

- ■ *Discuss confidentiality openly with the parent and child (as is age appropriate) before others are brought in*

  - Explain the concept of confidentiality.

  - Explain the limits of confidentiality (in terms of both nonprofessionals and professionals—the agencies involved should have their own policies around confidentiality).

  - Help them weigh the benefits versus the harm of including certain participants in visitation, in light of possible breaches of confidentiality.

  - Have them identify any topics that are particularly sensitive and that they would like protected.

  - Have them help you draft guidelines around confidentiality for their visits.

  - Give them veto power over inclusion of participants.

■ ***Discuss confidentiality openly with all participants, ensuring their understanding and gaining their concurrence***

- Explain confidentiality in concrete behaviors ("You must not tell anyone outside this room anything that happens here") to ensure that they understand what it means.

- Explain the unpleasant consequences for the parent and child when confidentiality is broken.

- Distribute and discuss guidelines drafted with the parent and child.

■ ***When breaches of confidentiality occur, handle this openly***

- Explore why it happened to see if it can be avoided in the future.
- Explain the harm that was done by the breach, with the offended party specifically stating feelings or other repercussions.

- Have the team decide if the offending party should discontinue involvement with visitation, with the offended person having a major voice.

Full Disclosure

Full disclosure has always been an issue in child welfare, but it has taken on new importance in light of ASFA and its emphasis on concurrent planning. Thus, when data are being gathered to consider simultaneously the feasibility of reunification and the possibility of TPR and adoption, the family needs to understand this process. It becomes increasingly important that they understand what is expected of them in terms of behavior changes, the timelines for achieving these changes, and the consequences for failure to achieve the changes. They also need to know about any appeals processes to which they are entitled.

Another aspect of full disclosure relates to recording. Client access to records was a much-discussed issue in the 1960s. Though few clients have actually requested access to their records, inclusive practice and full disclosure would suggest that records should be written in such a way that the worker would feel comfortable sharing the information with the client (barring special confidentiality issues, such as third-party involvement). Writing for full disclosure, whether or not the client ever actually sees the record, can be a good reminder to workers to check out their perceptions and interpretations with families and to communicate their respect for the family through their recording.

Reasonable Efforts

Reasonable efforts, viewed as an ethical issue, is a complicated subject. As a legal issue it is clearly required, but specifics are lacking. As professionals who value family ties and want to support and strengthen them to the extent consistent with child safety and well-being (and barring the special circumstances discussed in ASFA), we feel an obligation to give families every opportunity to show that they can safely rear their children. This professional responsibility suggests that workers need to go beyond the letter of the law (vague though that may be), beyond perfunctory provision of reasonable efforts, and ask such questions as whether the services offered are acceptable to the family, culturally relevant, and accessible.

The greatest ethical dilemma concerns worker responsibility when adequate services are lacking. Should families lose their children because they are unfortunate enough to live in low-resource areas? At this point, the question is more one of societal ethics than of worker ethics. The best resolution for the worker is to make service needs known and to advocate for services that may allow families a fair chance in achieving the terms of their case plans and resuming parenting of their children when appropriate.

Table 2. Guide to Planning for Visitation

Variables/ Dimensions	Overriding Issues/Factors					
	Safety	Permanency Goal	Stages, Time in Care	Family, Culture	Age of Child	Handling Logistics
Timing: • how soon • how often • duration			Move toward 2/wk. in a month		3-yr.-old, start 1st week, 1 hour	
Place: • child's home • foster home • agency • center • natural env. • profess. appt.	Foster home 1st visit, until safety assured		Move toward home and other later			
Participants: • father • siblings, pets • other relatives • friends • professionals	Mother only at 1st (BF questionable)		Assess BF later	GM important to family		GM transportation problems; tokens?
Content: • attachment • parenting • child development • decision-making		Reunification, all content needed	Month 2, assess progress in each area	Spanking issues	Focus on discipline for 3-year-old	
Controls: • secure place • observation • supervision • rules	Rules around BF attending	Observation regarding parenting skills	Later reassess BF			

Note: BF = boyfriend; GM = grandmother

Summary

In this chapter we have examined some of the basic variables and issues that should be considered in planning and implementing visitation. We have seen that decisions must be made concerning a range of interrelated variables or dimensions of visitation and that these decisions are made within a context of other factors. Table 2 presents this information in a format that may be used as a guide to planning for visitation.

Not all cells in Table 2 need to be filled in, but each should be considered. Some of the cells have been completed here to demonstrate how the table might be used.
The worker may use this grid with other participants to determine initial and ongoing answers to their planning questions (e.g., "Where might visits best take place, in consideration of the child's safety needs, permanency goal, time in care, familial and cultural considerations, and age? And does the agency have or can the agency and family together acquire the resources to support this choice?").

We have seen how visitation planning might require special consideration when a child is in kinship care, the importance of visitation when a child is in group care, and the role of visitation when a child has been adopted. We have explored some of the obstacles to visitation when a parent is incarcerated. Last, we have examined ethical issues related to confidentiality, full disclosure, and reasonable efforts.

Attending to these issues, variables, and special considerations during initial planning and ongoing review of visitation sets a structure that will go far in determining the success of visitation. The next chapter delves more deeply into the content of visits, exploring ways that the time parent, children, and other participants spend together will be most productive and most apt to ensure child safety, permanency, and well-being.

Strategies for Improving Visitation

The previous chapter described a number of issues and variables involved in visitation. This chapter will look more closely at the content of visitation and how participants' time together can be used to produce the optimal visitation experience and optimal benefits. The strategies presented here represent "best practice" for visitation. But before examining specific strategies, several principles concerning visitation are offered. These set the context for considering and choosing appropriate strategies, which may be seen as more specific expressions of these principles. Any strategies chosen or decisions made regarding visitation should be consistent with these principles. In addition, a general process for planning and implementing the initial visit will be described—a process that, with modifications, can be the model for subsequent visits.

Principles

The following principles guide good practice in relation to visitation:

1. **Visitation is sacrosanct.**

   Visitation is so important to the child's safety, permanence, and well-being that it is always to be supported unless there is a compelling reason to the contrary. Even when safety is an issue, every effort should be made to handle the safety issues through controls around visitation rather than through discontinuing visits. Visits should never be used as bargaining chips, reward, or punishment for a parent or child.

2. **Decisions and conclusions based on participant behaviors in relation to visitation must reflect a deep understanding of the emotional impact of separation and visitation and deep empathy for all participants.**

   For instance, a parent's reluctance to visit should not be automatically viewed as disinterest but rather should be discussed with the parent in consideration of the emotional context.

3. **Visitation is a collaborative venture, inclusive in the broadest sense.**

   It may involve, for instance, nuclear family, extended family, community agencies, schools, and others. All participants (including the child at an age-appropriate level) need to understand the importance, purposes, challenges, and feelings about visitation; and all should have the opportunity to express their desires and preferences. The visitation plan emanates from and belongs to all significant participants, using the strengths, competencies, and expertise of all.

4. **Discussions around visitation should be characterized by openness and full disclosure of any relevant information.**

   This should include information about what outcomes and behaviors are expected of the parent and other participants, timelines for accomplishing the work of visitation and for achieving the permanency goal, feedback about how the participants are doing, consequences of not meeting expectations, and—if relevant—information about concurrent planning.

5. **Visitation needs support.**

   Visitation is an awkward arrangement, and how to negotiate visits is not intuitive. It is not a natural extension of ongoing parenting but rather a contrived situation. The worker should not expect any participants to know how to do it without much help, explanation, empathy, feedback, and emotional and logistical encouragement.

6. **Visitation planning should include an ecological perspective.**

   A child is attached to people, places, and things other than the primary parent. Thus, visitation planning should seek to maintain the child's connectedness to the extended family and neighborhood.

7. **Visitation planning is not static.**

   As situations change, as the worker's knowledge of participants changes, as the parent changes, as participants progress through the stages of visitation, changes in the plan are to be expected.

8. **Risk is an ever-present consideration, but there is almost always a way to control for risk without discontinuing visits.**

   Use the resources of all participants to determine the level of risk and specific risky situations and to find acceptable and effective controls.

9. **The core question in planning visitation is how decisions around particular variables (e.g., where, when, who) support the purposes of visitation for a particular family, and especially for a particular child, whose needs are primary.**

10. **Visitation should be used to support family ties, regardless of the permanency goal.**

    Visitation is the core service for maximizing ties and can be used to support negotiation of the future parent–child relationship whether or not the parent and child will ever live together again.

General Process

Most of the information presented here is not new, though it has been updated by emerging thinking and represented in legislation (e.g., Adoption and Safe Families Act [ASFA]) and ongoing efforts to improve practice. Thus, the process described here represents a gathering of and expansion upon some of the thoughtful work that has been undertaken over the past twenty years or so regarding visitation. One certainly cannot write in this area without crediting that good work, which is referenced throughout this publication.

Because there is such variation among agencies in configuration of the team or staff who are responsible for visitation, in this chapter the term "worker" is often used generically to refer to whoever may be in charge of particular functions.

Agency Support to Undergird Practice

Hess (1988 and 1999) has repeatedly addressed the need for agency support for visitation, by way of policies, resources, and practice standards to undergird practice. This has been discussed at length in Chapter 5 and will not be repeated here. The criticality of the full range of agency supports, however, cannot be overestimated.

The First Visit as a Model

Preparing for the first visit may be characterized as immediate, intensive, and intentful.

■ *Immediate*

Planning must be immediate, because practice standards normally recommend that the first visit come within a week of placement or sooner for very young children and infants, before the relationship begins to wither. This immediacy is also important in terms of the timelines of ASFA, as there is no time to lose in helping a family meet its permanency goals. Recognition of this immediacy can be motivating, as it communicates to participants the importance of visitation in a way that a more relaxed timeframe would not.

■ *Intensive*

Because so much work has to happen so quickly in planning for the first visit, preparation is very intensive, requiring concentrated blocks of time from the worker with various parties. It is worth putting great effort into making the first visit as successful as possible. Though the plan developed and recorded at this point will not be the plan that will serve as participants get to know one another better and as they move through time together, careful attention to detail at this point not only ensures success of the first visit but also sets a positive tone for future visits.

■ *Intentful*

From the beginning all participants need to understand visitation and its activities as serving the permanency goal and meeting other related purposes. Going from spending much of their time together to little, perhaps an hour a week at first, participants need to understand the preciousness of that time and that every minute spent together and every activity should be maximally used. The time cannot be squandered in ill-planned confusion.

What might immediate, intensive, intentful planning of the first visit look like? Here are some details, arranged in approximately the order in which they need to be considered (though the order will certainly seldom be exactly as presented here). Note that all of these activities are to be carried out collaboratively, with open discussion of opinions and preferences and with extensive sharing of information.

■ *At the point of separation talk about the first visit.*

Lay it out as an expectation and a task that participants will be working on together in the coming days. Model openness and problem solving as you anticipate difficulties and generate solutions.

■ *If visitation is addressed in the court order, use that as the basis for early planning and ensure that all participants know what is in the order.*

■ *Determine if the visit needs to be supervised or needs other restrictions and if so the extent of the supervision or restrictions.*

This relates primarily to safety issues and will influence many subsequent decisions (e.g., who, where).

■ *Decide who needs to be present at the first visit.*

At this point immediate contact between the parent and child is probably of primary importance, although in some instances siblings may be equally important. Yet, due to logistical difficulties and the high emotional state of the parent and child, fuller ecological planning will probably be part of later visits rather than the first.

■ *Decide on the place for the visit.*

Though the child's home is the preferred location, err on the conservative side at first—foster home, office, or other controlled setting—if safety is an issue.

■ *Arrange and coordinate transportation, child care, or other logistics (e.g., time, place, supervision, tasks) to support visitation.*

■ *Tend to the purpose of the visit.*

Though we have seen that visitation serves many purposes, the extent to which any one purpose will be met in the first visit may be limited. The most essential purpose during that visit will be to maintain the parent–child contact so that ties will not begin to fade, to begin to set a pattern for this particular kind of interaction that will be the groundwork for further work together and for meeting further purposes.

■ *Write it down.*

Regardless of how rudimentary the initial plan may be, write it down. Hess (1999) has repeatedly reported that visits are much more apt to take place if the visitation plan is written. In terms of good practice, arrangements around visitation are too complex and too important not to be written down.

■ *Distribute the plan to primary participants.*

Every primary participant should have a copy of the visitation plan. This serves as a reminder that visitation is a central service, serves as concrete evidence that contacts will continue and attachments will be supported, and provides a reminder of the logistical details of which all must be aware. In addition, it demonstrates planning and home organization for the parent, an important life skill. A simplified, age-appropriate version of the plan may be prepared for and given to the child. For instance, a very young child can understand a large-lettered board that shows a month's days of the week and a picture of Mommy on every Thursday, and the foster parent can help the child count down the days between and perhaps use the interim days to prepare a picture or something special for the occasion.

■ *Prepare all participants in terms of what will occur during the visit.*

Review logistics. Be sure participants understand such things as who will be there and any time limitation for the visit.

■ *Prepare all participants in terms of emotional readiness.*

This will be ongoing work, allowing and encouraging full exploration of participants' own feelings as well as any speculation they may make about others' feelings.

■ *Coach, rehearse, and troubleshoot.*

Generally participants lack the right words for implementing the first visit smoothly. As previously stated, visitation is an awkward situation exacerbated by high emotions. Parents will surely be wondering such things as, How do I explain why we are living apart? What do I do if my child rejects me? What do I say if the child asks when she can return home? What do I do if she clings and cries and will not let me leave? Children will also have their questions and fears. It is helpful to prepare parents and children to handle any difficult situations that may arise.

■ ***Provide reassurance that you will be available after the visit to help the participant with any questions or issues in relation to the visit.***

The parent and child need to know beforehand that the visit will not come off flawlessly. Despite the best coaching, there will be awkward moments, painful moments, wrong words spoken, misunderstandings, and disappointments mixed with the joy and relief at seeing one another again. The parent and child need to know that they will not be left to handle these things alone and that someone will be available to listen and help. Problems will not be left to fester and poison future visits but rather will be used productively, to deepen understanding and enhance skills. This reassurance can allow the parent and child to tolerate their own discomfort and can motivate them to see the visit through, despite the discomfort.

■ ***Be available at the time of the visit.***

You may have a supervisory role, but even if you do not it is important that you be available to tend to any last-minute glitches that may occur, thus ensuring that the first visit goes as smoothly as possible.

■ ***Follow through with your promise of availability after the visit.***

Debrief with all primary participants. Help them talk about feelings and concerns. Start building the web of empathy. And use the experience for looking toward the next visit.

■ ***Document.***

Essential facts of the visit as well as your assessment of those facts form the beginning of a record that will have important consequences for the family and their future lives together.

This list of tasks around the first visit may look overwhelming, but each step is necessary to ensure that visitation gets off to a good start. As shown in Figure 1, this is only one event cycle (anticipation, visit, aftermath) in a complex three-stage (early, middle, late) process involving many participants.

Fortunately, getting the first visitation right has enormous payoff. The pattern of how to accomplish visitation is set in the beginning, and the changes that must occur throughout the process should be an orderly extension of the initial cycle. Each of the aforementioned steps should be reconsidered in relation to each visit. Because some of the steps will be quickly checked and require no change (e.g., need for restrictions may be fairly well ruled out, transportation may be regular and dependable, expectations may be clear), the process of considering the steps will become easier with time.

Yet, one step will need ongoing attention as you proceed through the stages of visitation, and that is consideration of the purpose of the visit. Whereas the first visit may have taken a limited view of purpose (e.g., ensuring maintenance of relationship), subsequent visits must focus on other purposes, those tied to decisionmaking and achievement of the permanency goal. In addition, feedback provided during postvisit debriefings will likely supply information that will help shape the purpose of further visits.

In summary, visitation planning and implementation should be firmly rooted in certain principles, needs the full support of the agency, and should include consideration of the steps listed above. These steps represent a model for the first visit and also, with different emphases in different stages of work and with different families, a model for each subsequent visiting event. Following are more ideas about strategies for improving the quality and outcomes of visits.

Specific Strategies

This section presents strategies for improving visitation in relation to the following topics: visitation planning; monitoring, decisionmaking, and documenting; progressing through stages; working with emotions; and teaching parenting.

Visitation Planning

The need for careful planning around visitation cannot be overemphasized. Visitation planning cannot be left to happenstance, and the plan must be prepared collaboratively and must be written down.

Key Requirements

The key requirements for a visitation plan are *integrity* and acceptability. Integrity means that the plan is actually capable of producing the desired result. Thus, if we consider the permanency goal the primary desired result, the plan must be carefully linked to that goal. If, for instance, the goal is reunification, the worker must have good reason to think that the elements included in the visitation plan, if adhered to, will indeed result in reunification. Of course, sometimes the goal is not attained and has to be changed, but when that occurs it should be because the parent could not achieve the original goal or because of changed circumstances rather than because of a plan that lacked integrity.

Integrity may be particularly important in light of concurrent planning. Though the worker may not be 100% sure that reunification will be achieved, integrity demands that the plan prepared give the family the best chance to achieve the reunification goal.

There must be no halfhearted support for reunification just because other possible options are recognized. Thus, integrity relates to the content of the visitation plan, which must incorporate activities that provide opportunities for parents to learn, practice, and assess new skills.

Acceptability means that the plan must be acceptable to the family and must be consistent with family values, preferences, styles, and traditions. This is important not only because families deserve to have their differences respected but also to support compliance. Families are more apt to comply with a plan that is comfortable for them. Thus, the family's full participation is to be encouraged and enabled. Acceptability relates to the process of visitation planning. The worker elicits all the information he can from the family about the full range of visitation issues. Are there religious holidays on which it is particularly important for the family to be together? Are there older, venerable family members that must be included? Is there a particular night of the week when a family dinner together has taken on special significance?

Content of the Plan

What should be included in a visitation plan? This should be determined by a blending of agency policy and practice guidelines and individual family needs and desires.

If agency policy and practice guidelines are adequate, they will set the framework for content of the plan. They may dictate both what elements must be addressed and certain minimum requirements. These elements have been discussed in the previous chapter and were summarized in Table 2. The plan should be driven first by consideration of safety and the permanency goal. The following elements should be addressed:

- timing (e.g., how soon, how often, duration),

- place (e.g., child or parent's home, foster home, agency, center, natural environment, park, restaurant, recreational activities, school, professional appointment),

- participants (e.g., father, siblings, pets, friends, professionals, other relations),

- content (e.g., attachment, parenting child development, decisionmaking), and

- controls (e.g., secure place, observation, supervision, rules).

Policy or practice guidelines (or, in their absence, professional standards) also should indicate minimal standards. For instance, Hess (1999) suggests that the first visit should be made within three days to a week, and subsequent visits weekly at a minimum but more often for infants and young children. As to location, many professionals suggest the first option is the child's (parent's) home unless there is a good reason to the contrary, because it provides privacy and lends some degree of normalcy to interactions. The plan should also be explicit concerning what the agency will provide logistically to support visitation, such as transportation, tokens, or cash to help purchase meals.

Activities should be related to individual family needs and desires. Some specific activities may be spelled out in the plan, still leaving room for flexibility as new opportunities and ideas emerge. Loar (1998) has suggested that there may be a need for structuring the visits, including a ritual greeting and good-bye as well as breaks in activities to accommodate the short attention spans of children. The potential range of activities is limitless, including such things as taking classes together at the Young Woman's Christian Association (YWCA), visiting parks and other recreational areas, or visiting libraries (Loar, 1998).

Controls are almost invariably related to safety concerns. Besides relating to place and supervision, they may include special conditions, such as remaining sober, not making promises, not making threats, refraining from touch (particularly in relation to sexual abuse), or not bringing certain companions along (Hess, 1999).

Process of Preparing the Plan

We have said that full involvement of participants not only affords families the respect they are due but also supports compliance. Only open and ongoing conversations with the family will unearth the details of their lives—their values, traditions, habits, styles of interaction—that can produce a plan that is truly theirs. In addition, in the long run it is a much more efficient use of time to initially create a plan that is acceptable to the family and that uses their full intelligence and creativity than it is to produce an inadequate plan that crumbles during implementation and has to repeatedly be rewritten (or, worse, the family is labeled as noncompliant).

Collaborative planning involves four essential worker activities:

■ **Including the relevant people**

For example: parent and child at a minimum and others as indicated—relatives, professionals, foster parents.

■ **Asking the right questions or exploring the right topics**

For example: asking what the parent wants out of visit, what she would like to do, how much time she would like to spend, where she would like to go, and asking the child what she would like to do and where she would like to go.

■ *Listening to their responses*

For example: asking for clarification as needed, repeating their words to ensure understanding, asking for more information, finding and supporting the sense in any idea, uncovering intent.

■ *Negotiating solutions as needed*

For example: meshing policy, practice guidelines and professional standards with idiosyncratic family needs and desires to arrive at solutions that have maximal integrity and acceptability.

Collaborative planning may occur between only two people (e.g., worker and parent) or with a larger group (e.g., family group planning), but the essential process is the same as described here.

Last, ensure that the plan is given to each participant as appropriate—at least to the parent and child. It is also helpful to include some sort of aides, particularly for children, so they can keep track of the plan (e.g., a calendar to keep track of visits; for parents a format for recording their satisfaction, accomplishments, and issues).

Teams, Roles, and Coordination

As we have seen, there may be many participants in visitation. Some have limited roles (e.g., perhaps friends or relatives who are only periodically included), whereas others have ongoing and significant roles in not only planning and implementing but also in preparing, giving feedback, and assessing. This core of people is sometimes referred to as the visitation team. In working with a team, some of the issues that must be addressed are the functions of the team, whom to include, roles of various participants, and coordination.

Functions of the Team

The overall function of the team is to ensure that the family is progressing satisfactorily toward the permanency goal. To do this, they will

■ meet together at some regularly scheduled times;

■ brainstorm about the purposes of visitation, needs, and resources;

■ see that all relevant information is brought to bear on the team efforts;

■ develop the visitation plan;

■ assign roles and responsibilities;

■ monitor ongoing implementation;

■ identify and address obstacles;

■ review and revise the plan as indicated;

■ assess goal achievement and the need for changing a permanency goal; and

■ support one another throughout.

These are essentially the functions that would be expected of a lead worker. And although the ultimate responsibility for visitation, as with other aspects of the case, may lie with the worker, sharing duties and responsibilities among participants who have an investment in the outcome brings information and resources to the family that otherwise may go unrecognized.

Whom to Include

There is great variety in who is included on teams, related to individual family characteristics and situations as well as to the agency's use of external resources (e.g., private agencies, other public agencies). At a minimum the team should include the parent, child, foster parent(s), and the public agency worker; but it may also include private agency workers, treatment providers, extended family members, and others. Particularly when the placement is kinship care, the team might include a family therapist or other professional who is familiar with family dynamics, such as triangulations, boundaries issues, and coalitions (Lee and Lynch, 1998).

In deciding how inclusive to be, the worker and family should consider such things as the

■ specific contribution each person can make,

■ balancing the benefits of inclusiveness against logistical difficulties,

■ family desires as to whom they would like to have there, and

■ confidentiality issues.

The team may decide to define a core who will participate regularly and to call in others as needed or desired.

Roles of Participants

For a team to work effectively, members need to know their roles. Though roles will depend to some extent on the particular family and its circumstances (e.g., who has what time, skills, material resources such as an automobile), the agency also holds basic expectations of core team members (Hess, 1999). It is important to remember that participants do not automatically know their roles nor do they know how to function as team members. Thus, the agency must offer orientation and training if they are to expect participants to carry out their roles effectively.

Usually the child welfare worker will function as the leader of the team. He will arrange and facilitate team meetings; represent agency and professional standards to the team in relation to all decisions; take ultimate responsibility for the plan, preparing and distributing the written form; oversee plan implementation, ensuring that all logistics are running smoothly and that progress is being made; ensure safety; supervise as needed; meet with individuals as needed around preparation for visits and after-visit discussions; ensure that all team members understand, are trained for, and are implementing their roles productively; ensure that service providers not represented on the team are nonetheless part of the information exchange; document; testify in court and provide information at any other required reviews; and ensure through supervision and ongoing professional development his own competence.

Frequently the agency contracts with private agencies to manage visitation or some aspect of visitation. In that case, many of the functions described for the child welfare worker will actually fall to the private agency worker. If this is the case, however, it is extremely important that an effective mechanism for reporting back to the child welfare worker be in place.

The child's parent, because of her great investment in the outcome of visitation and because she is the focus for change, must be supported in accepting ownership and a sense of responsibility for visitation. She must attend all meetings, understand and accept visitation as the primary mechanism through which she will work toward the permanency goal, explore resources she can bring to bear on visitation, participate meaningfully in planning, implement the plan as designed, openly discuss her reactions with the worker and the team, readily discuss and participate in the resolution of any obstacles or conflicts, and participate in required court or other reviews.

The child also may have a role, depending on her developmental level. The child may be present at meetings as appropriate (balancing the need for involvement, ability to understand, and ability to contribute). Children struggling valiantly with their own emotional reactions and their need to continue their developmental progression do not need to be saddled with the responsibility for visitation, but their opinions need to be sought. Older children and adolescents certainly need to be consulted and may be included in negotiations concerning scheduling and content of visits. This process can decrease their feelings of powerlessness as well as produce a plan that is more respectful of the child's ongoing life and activities outside the home.

An Erie County, Pennsylvania, study (1999) showed that, though most child welfare workers believe foster parents should be involved in the team (providing such things as education, mentoring, monitoring, hosting, and transportation), foster parents often do not feel accepted as part of the team. In addition, many believe they already have enough to do without accepting greater responsibility for visitation. This indicates both that the agency needs to be clear about its expectations of foster parents and that open discussions need to take place about how foster parents see their role in relation to these expectations.

Certainly foster parents should be included as part of the team, because their role in supporting the ongoing relationship between the parent and child is central. It is they who are there day to day with the child to support the child's positive perception of the parent, note ongoing child difficulties that may need to be addressed by the team, and spend time with the child before and after visits. In addition, they can act as positive role models for the parent, providing ongoing, hands-on parent education in an informal, home environment. Thus, they both have valuable information to provide for the team and can use information that they learn from others to better care for the child and work with the parent. Some foster parents have become so important to not only the parent but also the extended family that their involvement has continued long after a child's return home.

Coordination

Families' service plans can be very complex, involving referrals for such things as mental health counseling for the parent or child, family therapy, alcohol and other drug counseling, and parenting classes. The parent or child may also be involved with school counseling or special education services, medical providers, corrections or juvenile justice services, sexual abuse offender counseling, family violence services, or services to enhance employment.

Everything that occurs in relation to these services relates to how the parent and child will eventually live together in a situation that ensures child safety, permanence, and well-being. Thus, it also relates to visitation, the ultimate testing ground for the effectiveness of other services. An important role of the child welfare worker as team leader is to be the manager of two-way communication between the team and these other providers (who may or may not be ongoing team participants).

Monitoring, Decisionmaking, and Documenting

There is good reason for why we have chosen to address these three topics together. Though decisions concerning visitation (where, whom to involve, controls) are continually being made, perhaps the most important decision concerns the permanency goal: whether reunification continues to be a realistic goal (or if the permanency goal needs to change) and when to reunify. The basic question is, "Has the parent demonstrated that she can safely parent the child?" But that question cannot be answered without careful ongoing monitoring, and the results of that monitoring must be documented as part of a recommendation to the court for reunification or change of the permanency goal.

These three activities are so interrelated that separating them for discussion is artificial. Thus, there is much overlap in the following discussion of these as there is in actual practice.

Monitoring

Monitoring is an ongoing process of gathering information according to some predetermined plan. The purpose is to ensure treatment integrity and acceptability by continually assessing fidelity to the plan (process monitoring), progress toward the permanency goal (outcome monitoring), and family satisfaction. Monitoring is important particularly in terms of ASFA timelines, because participants need to know how they are doing so they can address any obstacles immediately. Failure to monitor adequately can leave families facing time limits without having made sufficient progress.

Developing the mechanism for monitoring should be part of visitation planning. Thus, the mechanism should be developed with the family and whoever else is involved in the visitation team as appropriate. They should own the monitoring plan as much as they own the visitation plan, and the monitoring plan can form the basis on ongoing team discussions around visitation. It should reveal any problems the family is having in complying with the plan or any failure of the plan (lack of plan integrity) to result in achievement of the permanency goal. Thus, visitation plan revisions can quickly be made to better accommodate the family and help them work toward the permanency goal. Monitoring will also reveal when the team's best reasonable efforts are not resulting in achievement of the permanency goal and when that goal needs to be reconsidered.

Because monitoring is used as the basis for plan revision and for decisionmaking, it is important to consider not only what information is collected but also how it is interpreted. This implies always looking for the reasons behind behavior. For instance, a parent's late arrival, arriving with friends and interacting with them rather than the child, or making unrealistic promises to the child are important to note but should be explored in terms of parent dissatisfaction with the plan or other emotional issues rather than immediately assumed to be a lack of interest (Beyer, 1999b). The family must be intimately involved in exploring and interpreting their own behaviors.

The monitoring plan should include both process and outcome markers that indicate progress toward child safety, permanency, and well-being. A monitoring plan can never include everything we might be interested in knowing about, so the visitation team has to make choices about what is most important. This would include the following:

■ **Specific tasks**

Tasks may include such things as when visits are to occur, projections of when supervision should diminish or cease, and involvement in other services.

■ **Success criteria**

These are specific and observable behavioral indictors (both interim and final) that the family is progressing satisfactorily (e.g., parent can engage the child in play for thirty minutes without raising her voice, parent can feed and bathe her infant without assistance, or therapists reports that the parent is reliable in taking medication for depression and no longer resorts to alcohol). Criteria should reflect forward movement in relevant areas of parenting and a decreasing need for supervision. Criteria should be related to the specific problems the family was experiencing that brought the child into care. Final success criteria should reflect behaviorally what child safety, permanency, and well-being would look like for this particular family (child safely spends three consecutive weekends at home with parent without supervision). Safety is always included in the monitoring plan.

■ **Clear timelines**

Process timelines can easily be determined and included in the plan. Though it is impossible to know initially when parent's will achieve certain success criteria (outcomes), ASFA timelines force us to make reasonable projections, allowing participants to know when meeting those timelines may be problematic, and to decide on corrective action (e.g., plan revision, change of goal, or documentation of legitimate need to extend the timelines).

Decisionmaking

As we have said, though decisions around visitation are continually being made, the most important decision concerns the permanency goal: whether reunification continues to be a realistic goal (or if the permanency goal needs to change) and when to reunify. A well-designed and implemented monitoring plan and well thought-out interpretation of the facts provides the information for decisionmaking. This is not easy, though, because gathering and interpreting information from multiple sources and blending multiple perspectives is a complex activity. Caution must especially be taken in using difficult visits (e.g., missed visits, disruptive visits) as indicators of a parent's lack of interest and for proceeding to TPR (Loar 1998). Decisionmaking is the final drawing of conclusions based on this information and implies committing to a recommendation.

By the time a decision has to be made to return a child home or to change the permanency plan, it should come as no surprise to participants. Parents and others would have had ample opportunity to recognize and correct noncompliance and to know whether adequate progress was being made toward correcting any problems averse to child safety, permanency, or well-being. If reunification continues to be the plan, the family will already have demonstrated their ability to progressively care for the child safely. If the plan must be changed, the reasons for this will already be clear to all (though the actual decision still may come as an emotional shock).

It should be stressed that, though decisionmaking is a team activity and multiple perspectives of participants are to be considered, the ultimate responsibility for making a recommendation to the court lies with the child welfare worker. Yet, if monitoring has occurred as it should, the recommendation will be fairly clear and well supported.

Documenting

It is often said, "If it isn't documented, it doesn't exist." Of course this statement is not literally true, but it contains just enough truth to underscore the importance of documentation. Thus, concerning documentation, our suggestions are as follows:

- **Do it**

  Particularly when monitoring of visitation is done by someone other than the primary child welfare worker, it is important to establish some mechanism for regularly getting information to that worker for inclusion in the case record. The record then becomes available to all parties as a working document and is available for court where it supports the permanency recommendation and provides documentation of reasonable efforts and any other requirements.

- **Know what to record**

  Monitoring provides the information that needs to be recorded.

- **Show respect**

  It is easy to lapse into judgmental and pejorative language (e.g., the house was filthy, the mother was stubborn) in documenting. Consciously using respectful language in documenting is important primarily because it supports respectful thinking. In addition, it is useful to give the family portions of our documentation as a show of respect and to ensure that all are working from the same information.

- **Document accurately**

  There is much emphasis on being accurate, particularly in relation to recording for the court. Verifiable facts are to be recorded, and it must be clear what is fact and what is interpretation of facts or professional judgement. Though verifiable facts are extremely important and form the basis for documentation, they have limitations. What do those verifiable facts mean? Too often this meaning is provided by the worker without adequate consultation with other participants.

As these suggestions indicate, there is a difference between factual (what happened) recording and valid (true reflection of reality) recording. For instance, it may be a fact that Ms. Smith's visits began to decline after the first several visits, dwindling to about once a month. Still, validity demands that participants consider what this behavior might mean (e.g., Ms. Smith lost interest in her child; logistical problems prevented visits; Ms. Smith was depressed; Ms. Smith came to believe her child was better off without her; she was intimidated by the foster parent or other observer; or she decided she would never get her child back, so there was no use in visiting). We need to question the validity of our recording when we interpret facts in isolation and without appreciation of the multiple voices and multiple perspectives of participants.

How do we improve the validity of our recording? This requires maximal participation of those affected, offering their unique familial, cultural, or professional understanding of events. It also involves negotiating meaning, thinking together about the multiple perspectives, trying on different meanings, and stretching the thinking of all participants. All then emerge with a deeper understanding of events, as meaning is not only discovered but created through conversation. Thus, negotiating around documentation is a learning opportunity for everyone. With this process the worker does not relinquish responsibility for finally deciding what to record, but the documentation will be richer, fuller, and more closely aligned to reality.

Progressing Through Stages

Visitation may be conceptualized as proceeding through stages. Though there is no clear number of stages and there are no clear dividing lines between stages, it is helpful to think of at least three overlapping stages—early, middle, and late. Each has its own characteristics in terms of tasks, emotions, and accomplishments. We cannot say definitely how much time should be spent in each stage, but certainly they should be fitted into ASFA timelines. The worker should educate the visitation team and particularly the parent about these stages, because this will help them assess their progress.

Early Stage

When a child has just been placed and preparations are being made for the first visit, to occur as soon as possible but certainly within the first week, the immediate concerns are around safety, handling emotional reactions, and setting the tone for future visits. Tasks to support these concerns have been presented earlier in this publication. The child needs permission to settle into the foster home, and emotions need to be well enough under control so that visits can actually occur without undue trauma. The rawness of the emotions related to separation will be recognized and dealt with. After a few weeks the worker might expect that

- participants will understand the importance of visitation,

- safety issues will have been resolved or controlled for,

- a pattern of compliance with the initial plan will have been established, and

- beginning strategies for coping with the emotional upheaval will have emerged (for both the parent and child).

Middle Stage

The family then moves into the middle stage. They are settled into a pattern for visitation that is goal-directed. Though pain and other emotions are still present, they are under control to the extent that the real work of visitation can proceed. The focus is on tasks, and the integrity of the visitation plan is put to test. During this stage, the following should take place:

- Parents should be learning new ways to relate to the child and new parenting skills, while other parent and child difficulties are simultaneously being addressed.

- The parent and child, as well as others, will participate in ongoing monitoring of both the process and progress. In other words, participants must look at not only compliance with the plan but also if the parent and child are both improving (Hess 1999).

- The plan will be revised to reflect obstacles, changes, and parental progress. If all is going well, restrictions will be removed, duration of visits will be extended, and new people and places will be added to the visitation plan strengthening the child's connection to her ecology.

- Joint decisionmaking occurs throughout this stage. If the permanency goal needs to be changed, this can add an extra element to this stage as participants readjust their thinking and deal with emotions and logistics related to the new plan.

- The family's accomplishments should have been clearly demonstrated (by the end of the middle stage), and participants should be ready to change their focus to the actual transition to reunification or some other permanency arrangement.

Late Stage

This is the transition stage. Workers often omit this stage, which can result in reunification before a family is fully prepared and can threaten the stability of the reunification. If the goal is reunification, the tasks, emotions, and accomplishments of the late stage include

- demonstrating through extended unsupervised weekend visits that the child can be safely parented at home;

- consolidating of gains, helping participants understand what was accomplished and rejoice in their achievements;

- anticipating possible problems associated with the parent and child living together again and rehearsing solutions;

- supporting the parent's ability to self-assess and seek help before crises occur;

- discussing the emotional impact of reunification, including possible ambivalence as the parent once again faces the hard work of parenting;

- discussing any future relationship with the foster parents; and

- discussing any ongoing service needs to ensure stability of the reunification.

Working with Emotions

Chapters 3 and 4 of this publication have emphasized the centrality of emotions to visitation—the pain associated with separation and the myriad of emotions associated with visitation events (anticipation, the visit, and aftermath) and stages (early, middle, and late). Figure 1 (page 22) was introduced to depict the complexity of these emotions and emotional interactions among participants in visitation. In addition, it was said that understanding and managing these emotions is critical to sensitive, humanist, and effective visitation that can achieve permanency goals with families. Indeed, if emotions are unrecognized and not attended to, they can overwhelm participants and undermine any attempts to move forward in working on goals. On the other hand, if they are understood and used appropriately, they have an important role in supporting progress.

Building the Web of Empathy

Chapter 4 introduced the concept of building a web of empathy to describe the process of helping all participants understand their own feelings and the feelings of other participants. Note that it is not enough that the worker feel and express empathy; visitation can be undermined unless all participants learn to feel and express empathy (which is always an important life skill and certainly an important parenting skill).

Building the web of empathy can be furthered in individual sessions with participants, such as previsit and postvisit sessions, or in team meetings. In any case, the process involves the same basic steps:

- ### *Support participants, regardless of behavior*

   It is hard to give empathy before one has experienced it. Particularly when emotions are raw and lead to inappropriate behavior (e.g., pain and anger leading to attacks on the worker and foster parent), the tendency is to focus on the inappropriate behavior rather on the meaning and to counterattack or harshly correct (not what we want to model for parents). The participant, overwhelmed by his own emotion and feeling attacked by the worker, will be concerned only about defending himself, not about developing empathy. Alternatively, recognizing and legitimizing the feelings (pain and anger) has a calming effect, removes the need for defensiveness, and leaves the participant more open to exploring meaning. The worker might use words such as, "From the strength of your anger, I'm guessing this visit is really meaningful to you." It may also help to recognize the difficulty of the visitation for all concerned, that all team members have difficulties and strong feelings around visitation: "None of us knows quite how to act here, and we're all going to make mistakes."

■ *Help participants look at the meaning of their own behavior*

Once participants feel accepted and understood, they are more able to look at their own behavior and the meaning that lies behind the behavior. They may also learn to accept themselves (the legitimacy of their feelings and the reality of their behavior) more comfortably. The result of this is greater comfort with themselves (again, less defensiveness, less blaming others, more reality) and more energy to give to others. To promote self-understanding, the worker might use such language as, "What are you really feeling when you pull John up by his arm?" or "When you are late for visits, I know there must be a good reason. What do you think that might be?"

■ *Help participants think about the meaning behind the behavior of others*

Once participants feel accepted and gain some experience in looking at the meaning behind their own behavior, they are ready to apply that same skill to understanding the behavior of others. The worker might support this in language such as, "Marvin must have really been feeling awful to have pulled away as he did. What do you think is going on?" If the parent has trouble coming up with legitimate explanations, the worker might gently offer additional meanings, such as "Is it possible that he was angry because you were not able to make the last visit?"

Developing empathy does not happen all at once—it is a lifelong process—and everyone has different potential and moves at a different rate. Yet, the worker should look for every opportunity in conversations with participants—and there will be many opportunities—to use the words that further empathy. It should become almost second nature in team meetings and a part of every previsit and postvisit session.

Following is a typical visitation situation in which emotions are obviously aroused:

Ms. Linder, arriving one hour late for her first visit with her eight-year-old son, John, in the home of foster parent Ms. Sikes, apologized to neither John nor Ms. Sikes but rather began to berate Ms. Sikes for the way John's hair had been cut, shorter than his usual length. Ms. Sikes, a very good foster parent, taken aback by this attack, tried to stay calm, while explaining that his hair needed cutting and that Ms. Linder's tardiness had caused John much grief. During this exchange, John sat quietly in a big stuffed chair, with a sullen look. When his mother came over and ran her fingers through his hair, commenting that it was too short, he pushed her hand away and said, "Leave me alone."

This scenario offers an opportunity to work with each participant, separately or as a group, to better understand what happened. There is something to support in everyone's behavior (e.g., Ms. Linder's investment in her son's appearance, Ms. Sikes's understanding of John's reactions, and John's refraining from overt attacks despite his pain). And certainly everyone's feelings are understandable and legitimate. But each person needs a better understanding of his or her own behavior and an understanding of the others' feelings if future visits are to run more smoothly. The worker can talk about the episode as a learning experience for all, giving it a positive spin rather than a discouraging and negative connotation.

Ongoing Management of Reactions

Though building the web of empathy begins with the first visit, ongoing management of emotional reactions is also necessary. The worker can expect the rawness of emotional reactions to soften as participants settle into a routine, but the reactions do not disappear. They continue, as each visit reenacts the original separation. In addition, as new crises occur (e.g., a setback for the parent that leads to substance use), circumstances change (e.g., the parent moves and logistics are upset), the permanency goal is changed, or as families enter the later and transitional stage of visitation, new emotions arise. These emotions need to be dealt with in anticipation of visits, during visits, and in postvisit sessions. Following are some tips.

■ ***Prepare all participants before the first visit.***

Discuss emotions honestly and openly, including what all participants might feel. This approach communicates a shared investment in the family and it universalizes the emotions, adding to their legitimacy. This also communicates that the emotions are understood and thus can be controlled. Anger, withdrawal, and hurt are expected parts of the process and will change eventually. Thus, for instance, the mother who can anticipate her child's ambivalence stands a better chance of being able to contain her hurt and of not panicking during the visit.

■ ***Set behavioral expectations.***

Before the initial visit and others as appropriate, let participants know the standard of behavior. Discuss openly that their feelings will tend to get in the way of these behaviors, but that they are able to control their behavior. Clearly differentiate between the legitimacy of emotions and the acceptability of behavior. All feelings are to be respected and legitimized, but some behaviors (e.g., blaming, arguing, criticizing, hitting) will seriously undermine the success of the visit.

■ **Help everyone focus on the needs of the child.**

It is easy for participants to get caught up in their own emotions and to forget the central purpose of visitation, which is to further safety, permanency, and well-being for the child. For instance, participants need to be helped not to use the visits to act out their anger or pain but, if it must be done, to do that in the safer environment of a postvisit session. Note, though, that parents may not be able to contain their emotions if the worker has not begun the "web of empathy" work of accepting and legitimizing their emotions.

■ **Respect the child's emotions as you would any other participant.**

Respecting the child's emotions (e.g., pain, anger, feelings of disloyalty to the parent) implies both that we legitimize them and that we help the child get them under control, just as we would an adult. It is important to avoid letting our well-placed empathy for a child actually communicate disrespect by implying that we do not believe the child is capable of understanding and controlling emotions.

■ **Be attentive and responsive to the child's ongoing postvisit reactions.**

Frequently foster parents report that a child has emotional and behavioral problems following a visit. This may be anything from sadness, crying, anxiety, or defiance to inability to sleep alone, lapses in toilette training, nightmares, suicidal ideation, and self-mutilation. It may occur only in the hours or days just following a visit or may become more persistent, interfering with a child's daily activities and ongoing development. It is important that the worker and foster parents (and other team members as appropriate) not use these reactions as a sign that visits should be discontinued but rather assess them accurately. Participants need to consider if the reactions go beyond the normal grief reaction, what the behavior is communicating (e.g., conflicting loyalties, problems in the visits, problems in the parent-child relationship), and how to respond to the child's needs (Hess, 1999).

■ **Be attentive and responsive to the parent's ongoing reactions to visitation.**

The parent's strongest reactions to visits may be limited primarily to early visits or may otherwise be circumscribed. On the other hand, the reactions may be more persistent and severe, significantly interfering with visits and signaling greater problems. When a parent has ongoing difficulty controlling behavior (e.g., comes to visits intoxicated, persistently misses visits, maltreats during a visit, verbally or behaviorally interacts inappropriately with the child, ignores the child), this needs to be taken seriously and carefully assessed, and appropriate intervention and assistance should be offered. The solution may be fairly simple (e.g., logistical problems related to transportation, work schedule, or child care) or may signal serious ambivalence. Interventions might include such things as checking out all logistics before each visit, beginning or reinstating supervision, limiting the length of visits, or changing the location (Hess, 1999).

■ *Deal with emotions during visits.*

Sometimes the child welfare worker, other professional, or foster parent will be present at visits and will be able to help participants deal with emotions during the visits. This is particularly helpful when the emotions threaten to disrupt the visit. Most important is that any intervention be accomplished with great respect. For instance, a parent's anger may be defused respectfully on the spot by the worker's calm acceptance of the reason for the anger, warm nonverbal behavior, refocusing on the child, and promising to talk more about the parent's feelings after the visit. Likewise, a sullen child may be comforted by a supportive touch, recognition of the legitimacy of the hurt and pain, or encouragement and help in expressing feelings, concerns, wants, and needs.

■ *Deal with reactions to reunification.*

In the late stages of visitation, when a family is preparing for reunification, do not be surprised by some ambivalence. Though this is the resolution all have been working toward, resuming the responsibility for full-time care of the child also poses new threats and challenges.

■ *Deal with reactions to changing the plan.*

When visitation has demonstrated that the parent cannot resume full-time care of a child and the permanency goal has to be changed, this is a time of crisis for the family. Even though they might have been fully prepared cognitively (e.g., through full disclosure around concurrent planning), it would be impossible to be fully prepared emotionally. Thus, the worker needs to be prepared to handle whatever disbelief, anger, bewilderment, or grief the parent and child might be feeling.

■ *Deal with your own and other participants' reactions.*

The child welfare worker, foster parents, and other services providers must recognize and address their own emotional reactions. Because they are all invested in visitation, they all have emotional reactions to how visits go. They want the visits to go well, and they experience some anxiety or discomfort before and during visits. Particularly when plans have changed, workers may experience a sense of failure and resist dealing with the parent and child about this. Again, recognizing that everybody—the entire visitation team—is affected by this can ease the discomfort, and everybody can use the team for support. The workers should also go to their supervisors for support.

Parenting: The Central Concern

Parenting and the effect of parenting on a child are the central concerns of child welfare. It is because of some parenting deficit (abuse or neglect) and the detrimental consequences for a child that most families come into the child welfare system.

Not surprisingly, then, most services offered to families in the child welfare system focus on parenting and the effects of parenting on a child. If a parent is referred for mental health services due to depression, it is because that depression is interfering with her ability to protect and rear her child. If she is referred for substance abuse treatment, it is because substance use has interfered with her parenting. Other referrals are to services dealing explicitly with parenting issues such as parenting classes, nurturing centers, or home visitation. Furthermore, a child's referral to mental health, medical, or other services is primarily to treat conditions resulting from parenting deficits.

Parenting is also the central concern of visitation. It is during visitation that whatever is gained through other treatment services is integrated and where parent–child interactions stand the ultimate test. This section will explore how visitation supports and teaches parenting. It presents a philosophy of parenting, provides a framework for teaching parenting behaviors, addresses building discipline and behavior management, addresses helping parents support their child's ongoing development, and suggests techniques for teaching parenting.

Philosophy of Parenting

We have said that most services for parents involved with the child welfare system relate to parenting issues. Yet, each service provider to whom a family is referred may approach parenting differently. The child welfare worker can enhance the effectiveness of other treatment services and help the parent pull together what she is learning by offering an integrated philosophy of parenting.

Combining ideas from therapy, therapeutic parenting programs, and parent training or education allows the emergence of an enriched idea of what effective parenting is. We are presenting this as a philosophy of parenting. Following are reasons why this philosophy of parenting is so helpful:

■ *A philosophy makes parenting more understandable.*

It helps explain why some actions are preferable to others and integrates parenting knowledge and skills that parents might have learned through such interventions as parent education classes, counseling, and other forms of treatment.

■ ***A philosophy can be the basis for the parent making her own decisions.***

A philosophy of parenting is empowering. When a parent has incorporated a philosophy of parenting, she will not be dependent on "experts" for parenting advice. Instead, she can discover the right actions based on a set of beliefs that guide action. Thus, parental independent decisionmaking becomes more efficient and effective.

Following are some elements of the philosophy of parenting:

■ ***Parenting is about a relationship. (Preserve it.)***

Parenting is built on relationship and sustained through relationship. Generally, preserving relationship is more important that managing some aspect of behavior.

■ ***Parenting is ongoing conflict resolution. (Expect it, solve it.)***

Because the parent and child are separate people living together in a close relationship, conflict is inevitable. Thus, the goal is not to avoid conflict but rather to learn productive resolution of conflict.

■ ***Parenting involves mutual influencing and growing. (Be open to it.)***

Parenting is a two-way relationship. The parent and child bring new experiences and challenges to one another, and each continues to change and mature.

■ ***Parenting builds discipline in parents as well as in children. (Treasure it.)***

Though we usually think of parenting as helping children learn discipline, in reality children bring new challenges to parents every day that require their learning increasing self-discipline. Thus, children teach parents discipline also.

■ ***Parenting, because it involves growth, also involves pain. (Tolerate it.)***

Growth is always painful, but maturity demands tolerating pain when it is in the service of growth. The pain is to be understood and used productively rather than avoided or covered with various forms of self-medication (e.g., substance use, acting out, compulsive behaviors).

■ *Parenting is about building rather than tearing down. (Enjoy it. Enjoy people-making.)*

Despite the pain, parenting involves joy. The parent–child relationship and the opportunity to help build a human being can contain much joy.

■ *Parenting is for the long term. (Focus on it. Win the war.)*

Though day-to-day difficulties demand attention, a long-term view can often provide the perspective that helps parents decide what is really important and thus make better decisions.

■ *Parenting is ongoing self-assessment. (Learn it.)*

Despite the plethora of information available concerning parenting, parenting remains to a great extent a learn-as-you-go activity. Certainly a parent will want to use whatever information she can to guide her, but it is through trial and error combined with meticulous self-assessment that true learning occurs.

■ *Parenting is being. (Become it.)*

One becomes a parent through a process of ongoing personal change, and parenting is an expression of who one is.

This philosophy has implications for teaching parenting (parent-building) in the context of visitation:

■ Although teaching parenting should aim for knowledge and skill acquisition, this is secondary to learning a process of self-examination that leads to increasing authenticity in the parent-child relationship. Thus, though it is not therapy, teaching parenting contains elements of something akin to therapy, as parents are challenged and supported in their process of self-examination and personal change.

■ Outcomes of teaching parenting include personal change in areas such as greater self-knowledge, greater self-acceptance, greater tolerance for and positive use of the pain of parenting, acceptance of conflict as normal and necessary to the growth process, and greater self-discipline and self-control. These personal changes form the basis for productive use of new knowledge and skills.

■ Parents need models who not only are solidly grounded in relation to the knowledge base and skills of parenting but also have themselves experienced and are open to experiencing personal growth through parenting and other relationships (including relationships with foster parents, children, and others).

Teaching Parenting

Parenting is no simple matter, as it involves a combination of knowledge, skills, and emotional competence. Thus, any approach to teaching parenting must consider parental strengths and deficits in all these areas. Unfortunately, much parenting education is misdirected because of the lack of a complete and accurate assessment (Loar, 1998). Though the focus of work with a parent may be a specific act (maltreatment that brought the family into the child welfare system), in most instances ensuring that the maltreatment will not be repeated and ensuring ongoing child safety, permanency, and well-being will require greater change than, for instance, learning that beating a child is not an appropriate behavior control strategy. The parent needs to learn how to have ongoing positive interactions with the child through relating to the child differently.

The parent needs to master the following steps that lead to positive interactions with a child. In assessing parenting ability and designing an intervention, the worker or team will want to consider parental strengths and deficits in each of these areas.

■ **Understanding the relationship between what the parent does and child behavior and development**

Child development is not a random process. Though there are always influences that are not under the parent's control, the parent has tremendous influence in shaping—through words, actions, and attitudes—the child. This message is empowering for parents (Beyer, 1999b), and understanding it is the basis for further change.

■ **Paying attention to cues**

Children continually provide behavioral cues (crying, sulking, approaching, asking questions) concerning what they want and need. The parent cannot respond appropriately unless she is attuned to those cues. Deficits in this area can be due to the parent's internal emotional noise (e.g., anxiety or depression that reduce her psychological availability), lack of knowledge of what to attend to (e.g., not knowing that the child's behavior is communicating some want or need), or environmental interference (e.g., poverty or dangerous neighborhood that reduces availability).

■ Interpreting cues

The parent not only must know what to attend to but also must be able to interpret cues accurately (e.g., what different sounds of an infant's cry might mean). Deficits in this area may be related to the parent's own emotional noise (e.g., inability to separate the child's needs from her own, misinterpretations based on her own history and memories) or lack of knowledge (e.g., individuality, developmental level of child).

■ Responding appropriately

Once the parent notices and interprets cues from the child, she needs to respond appropriately. Deficits in this area may include difficulty in regulation of emotions (e.g., emotional control, ability to tolerate anxiety and discomfort), an inadequate repertoire of responses (e.g., not knowing the right words or behaviors, such as the skills to talk courteously; following the child rather than leading; reading a book; playing games) or not knowing how to select the appropriate response (e.g., based on the child's individuality, the child's developmental level, or the situation).

■ Learning from interaction cycles

We have said that parenting involves trial and error. But trial and error teaches better parenting only if the parent is able to critique her efforts. Many parenting failures are the result of repetitions of ineffective behaviors (e.g., hit, then hit harder) rather than using feedback to continue effective interactions and discontinue ineffective ones. For instance, the parent needs to be aware of the differential effects of her efforts to control the child's play versus gently following the child. Then she needs to shape her future behavior to achieve the best results.

The worker can use a strengths-based approach to helping parents master these steps. For instance, to demonstrate the relationship between parental behavior and child responses, the worker can look for instances in which a parent speaks softly to a child and the child quietly complies. The worker may then point out to the parent how her own calmness was transferred to the child. To reinforce attending to cues, the worker might note an instance in which the parent answers a child's question the first time rather than waiting until the child is frustrated. It is especially important when a parent seems to have corrected some past error (e.g., instead of telling the child what toy to play with, lets the child choose from a toy box) that the worker not only point out the effective parenting but also verbalize that the parent is learning and can continue to learn.

Building Discipline and Managing Behavior

Professionals and parents need to be attuned to the distinction between building discipline and managing behavior. We have said that parenting is about building people and that it is about the long term. Yet, the issue that is more apt to be at the forefront of parents' minds as well as the focus of much parenting training is immediate "child behavior problems," which in reality are only the symptoms of interactional difficulties between the parent and child. Often child maltreatment is related to well-intended, misguided, desperate attempts of parents to manage behaviors and symptoms. This brings us to the issue of discipline (building internal controls for the long term) versus behavior management (reliance on external controls for the short term).

First, note that we are not using "discipline" to mean punishment, as it is often used. Rather, discipline is taken to mean an internal process of regulating one's own behavior according to some standards, usually internalized standards of the parents or other attachment figures. When a child has learned appropriate discipline, minimal external behavior management is necessary. Behavioral management techniques are actions used when discipline has failed.

Most of the children coming into foster care have been failed in that they were not provided the experiences necessary for development of discipline—consistent, ongoing, developmentally appropriate teaching within a loving relationship. They are more apt to have experienced unrealistic expectations, inconsistent demands, and confusion about both the parent's and child's needs. Thus, professionals attempting to assist foster parents in caring for these children and attempting to help birth parents relate more effectively to their children must address managing immediate child behavior problems, but they must do so within a context of building long-term discipline, without sacrificing their relationship.

Supporting Child Development Through Age-Appropriate Activities

Though child welfare's primary parenting concern is child safety, we also must consider child development (well-being). Children who have been abused or neglected typically show some developmental delays. In addition, our disrupting their lives and relationships through out-of-home placement can lead to further developmental delays. In other words, our legal and moral obligation to ensure child safety can also contribute to additional problems. But child welfare must, first of all, do no harm. That means that we must attend to ongoing development of the children in our care.

Thus, children's development cannot be put on hold while they are in foster care; and development proceeds best within the context of an attachment relationship. Both for that reason and to prepare the parent to support ongoing development, we need to teach parents about expectations at developmental levels and teach them interactions and activities that will support specific developmental strivings. This happens through visitation. Visitation planning, therefore, must include engaging the parent and child in activities that are specifically designed not only to be appropriate to the child's current developmental level but also to support moving to higher levels of development.

Techniques

The following techniques are suggested for teaching parenting in the context of visitation:

■ **Coach and rehearse with the parent before the visit.**

Anticipate what might occur, design appropriate responses, and rehearse them. Have the parent actually try out the words and behaviors until she feels comfortable. For example, anticipating that a young child might ask if she can go home with the parent, help the parent form words that communicate empathy with the child's concern, reassurance of the parent's continuing presence, and the reality that this is not yet known.

■ **Plan parent-child interactions that support parenting skills.**

These activities might include such things as feeding, grooming, fixing hair, bathing, helping with homework (Egan, n.d.).

■ **Plan parent-child interactions that support relationship and family connection.**

These activities might include such things as playing together, bringing photos or videotapes of family, telling family stories, celebrating (e.g., birthdays, holidays), or singing (Egan, n.d.).

■ **Plan parent-child interactions that support child development.**

The parent might play games that focus on certain skills, talk at an age-appropriate level about moral issues (e.g., cheating, stealing), or read labels in the grocery store with the child.

■ **Coach and model during the visit.**

Because the surest way to assess parenting is direct observation, the foster parent, child welfare worker, or other trained observer may be present during visits. Direct observation affords the opportunity for immediate feedback and correction as well as modeling of behaviors. It is most important, however, that this be done unobtrusively and without undermining or diminishing the parent in front of the child. For instance, the observer might correct the use of a rough tone of voice by demonstrating a quieter approach to the child; or he might lead the parent to more positive interactions by asking, "Would you like to try just watching Joshua for a minute and then following his lead, letting him show you how he wants to play?" When parental behavior is truly disruptive, the observer might request a time-out and gently lead the parent out of hearing distance of the child and help her calm down so the visit will not have to be terminated.

■ *Critique after the visit.*

It is helpful if visits can be videotaped; but if that is not possible, the visit can still be critiqued from the participants' (usually somewhat distorted) memory of the visit. The critique should

- communicate appreciation of the parent's expertise in knowing her own child;

- communicate appreciation of the parent's individuality, including styles and preferences (Beyer, 1999b);

- reinforce positives and avoid negative references, always recognizing positive intent despite ineffective or counterproductive behaviors;

- offer suggestions in a manner that communicates common exploration of approaches and techniques rather than criticism and correction; and

- connect to the principles of parenting discussed earlier.

Conclusion

This chapter has provided information intended to improve the quality and effectiveness of visitation. It presented principles to serve as overall guides to thinking about visitation, laid out the steps in a first visit, and provided specific suggestions regarding various aspects of visitation (planning; monitoring, decisionmaking, and documenting; progressing through stages; working with emotions; and teaching parenting).

This information relating to the content of visits is to be understood within the context of separation; the full emotional experience of visitation; contextual factors, such as law, policy, resource, and professional standards; and a variety of issues. Together, these elements provide a rich picture of what visitation can be.

Appendix A contains summary versions of much of the material that has been presented in this publication. These tools may be used by agencies to review their understanding of and support for visitation or by workers to guide their practice. They may also be used by any participants in visitation as appropriate. It is particularly important that the tools be introduced to parents and foster parents as appropriate, communicating to them that professional knowledge and skills are not to be jealously guarded but rather to be shared and given away whenever possible, truly empowering the entire visitation team.

Promising Programs
and Practices

A ny attempt to present promising programs and practices is necessarily frustrating, and one is always acutely aware that many fine examples have been omitted. Not only would it be impossible to review all such initiatives because of their number, but also many innovations are happily and quietly occurring without recognition or documentation. Still, it is useful to look at a few examples of current programs or practices that represent attempts to improve visitation services. Thus, to limit and structure this discussion, we have chosen to focus on programs and practices involving some sort of supervised visitation, an arena that is currently growing and has much potential for influencing practice in general. Though many centers and supervised visitation initiatives serve only separated or divorced families (substance-involved couples, domestic violence, or other high-conflict situations such as contested custody), others also serve or exclusively serve child welfare families. We are restricting our reporting here to this latter group of programs and practices.

A brief description of each of the programs or practices reviewed here is presented. But even more useful may be the tools that are referred to and are included as appendixes. These include various sorts of checklists, forms, or guidelines that may stimulate one's thinking and suggest elements that may be transferable to one's own visitation program.

Following is information on various initiatives:

■ *Catholic Charities Therapeutic Supervised Visitation Program*

This is only one program of many offered by Catholic Charities of Buffalo, New York. It is included as an example of a well-developed therapeutic program, to be distinguished from programs that may supervise visits but provide no or minimal treatment.

- ### *Starting Over: Saint Julian's Episcopal Church's Supervised Visitation Program*

  This program serving Douglas County, Georgia, is an example of a small, stand-alone church-based program developed as a ministry. It is important as a demonstration of the service that can be offered with minimal funding and a staff of volunteers.

- ### *The Family Visitation Center*

  This program in Colorado Springs, Colorado, is a good example of an initiative that arose from true collaboration among the public and private sectors and citizens of a neighborhood, who gave many hours of volunteer work to launch the program.

- ### *Neighborhood Foster Care*

  This initiative of the Casey Family Program and the Oregon State Office for Services to Children and Families is a good example of a comprehensive foster care program of which visitation is a part. This is an example of an initiative with a strong ecological emphasis and a focus on kinship care and sibling groups.

- ### *California Professional Society on the Abuse of Children*

  This is included because it provides good information and guidelines in relation to visitation when sexual abuse allegations are involved. Sexual abuse raises specific child safety concerns and calls for special therapeutic interventions and monitoring.

- ### *The Supervised Visitation Network (SVN)*

  SVN is an association of agencies and individual members who provide supervised visitation services. Though most providers serve primarily families experiencing separation and divorce, SVN also includes providers of services to the child protective services system. SVN is included here both because the organization should be considered an ongoing resource to the field of child welfare in terms of planning visitation for families when child safety is an issue and because it has developed standards that can inform child welfare practice.

Catholic Charities Therapeutic Supervised Visitation Program

This is a program of Catholic Charities of Buffalo, New York, which also operates a wide variety of related programs. The Therapeutic Supervised Visitation Program serves Erie County, New York, families involved with child welfare through protective services, out-of-home placement (primary users), or mandated preventive services if a supervised therapeutic visitation experience is warranted based on a court order or service provider recommendation. Users of the service include child protective services families in which safe access of a parent to her child must be assured during the investigation process, where there is risk of reabuse during contact; families with children in out-of-home care when the goal is reunification, particularly when family violence and substance abuse are involved; families involving children with special needs, such as alcohol and other drug (AOD) affected infants who have multiple handicaps and require special care; families in which chronic parental mental illness or other special needs are issues; and families using family preservation services and needing to learn parenting skills.

This program aims to prevent further maltreatment of children when safety is an issue, while ensuring ongoing contact between the parent and child and with other significant figures in the child's life. In addition, the therapeutic emphasis focuses on attachment issues, healing trauma, support for all parties, and teaching parenting skills through active intervention during visits. The program helps families work toward reunification, provides assessments as to their progress, and supports the transition to reunification. When returning home is not possible for a child, the program provides a healing environment as the family transitions to another permanency option. Staff also collaborate with all participants and other providers, and they integrate the therapeutic supervised visitation services with the overall service plan.

Each family referred to the program is assessed (collaboratively with the child welfare agency, visitation therapist, the family, and—as appropriate—foster family or placement facility) for safety, therapeutic intervention required, and parent education needed. All participants are oriented to the program, and children specifically are empowered to discuss their wants and needs in terms of visitation.

The visitation rooms are specially designed to meet the needs of the program. They are located centrally with bus transportation available. They are secure, furnished age-appropriately, configured to allow for conversation and a variety of play activities, and large enough to afford distance between the visitation therapist and the parent and child. The equipment includes a video camera and sensitive microphones. In addition, the sites have a reception area that is welcoming and includes security personnel, a conference room, and restrooms that can be monitored.

Visits can be arranged for weekdays and evenings (typically 9:00 A.M. to 8:30 P.M.) and weekends (typically from 9:00 A.M. until 4:00 P.M.). Visits are usually for one hour, once per week. Transportation for the child is provided by the foster family if possible. Parents provide their own transportation.

Therapeutic Supervised Visitation is a structured process geared to mobilize the child's and family's strengths, address the conditions that led to placement, offer healing, and involve significant others as appropriate. Changes in plans require collaboration and agreement by all significant participants. (When visitation is court ordered, the court is solely responsible for changes.) Movement toward less restrictive visitation is predicated upon successful completion of goals at each phase of visitation. Each visitation requires a previsit and postvisit period of 15 minutes with the parent or other significant participants to prepare for using the time to meet therapeutic goals.

The visitation therapist is responsible for maximizing visitation through such things as arranging logistics with the family, following up if visits are missed, addressing any problems, planning use of the time, and serving as a liaison with other professionals. Ultimate responsibility for the case rests with the department of social services (DSS) case manager, child protective services (CPS) worker, or other DSS employee as appropriate. All visits are monitored by a visitation therapist, and sessions are videotaped for supervisory and educational purposes. Evaluation is ongoing.

The program developed the following useful tools (see Appendix B):

■ *Catholic Charities of Buffalo, NY, Therapeutic Supervised Visitation Agreement, Policy Agreement*

Parents sign this agreement that specifies a code of conduct regarding visits, addressing such things as punctuality, cancellations, alcohol and other drugs, and limitations on behaviors and talking with the child.

■ *Catholic Charities of Buffalo, NY, Visitation Programs Observation Form*

The observer records on this form information related to parent–child interaction during the visit, activities, the child's mood and behavior, and any therapist intervention. In addition, there is a page that relates visitation goals to what occurred and to planning for the next session.

■ *Catholic Charities Visitation Performance Outcome Scale*

This scale allows for rating the parent's attachment, physical care of a child, provision of structure, communication, responsiveness to the child's needs, and healing (recognizing and dealing appropriately with child emotional trauma).

St. Julian's Starting Over Child Visitation Center

St. Julian's Starting Over Child Visitation Center, serving Douglas County, Georgia, was created specifically to address a need recognized by the Douglas County Juvenile Court for a safe, appropriate environment for visitation of families involved in child maltreatment, particularly when substance abuse and domestic violence are factors. The center, established in 1998, arose directly from the experience of the parish priest who had served as a supervisor for court-ordered visitation. It was conceived as an outreach program to offer supervised visits on the premises of the church.

St. Julian's Episcopal Church recognized that the child welfare agency, the Department of Family and Children Services, was responsible for supervising many more cases than it could handle and that the department, as well as the families it served, needed help. Thus, the program was begun as a resource to the court, the department, and families to offer space and volunteer supervisors to ensure that court-ordered visitations would actually occur.

Starting Over is considered part of the ministry of the approximately 400-membered St. Julian's Episcopal Church. The program mission statement reads, "Our mission is to assist families, where parent and child have been separated for various reasons by the court, get back together under a court-ordered supervised visitation program."

The program serves families referred from the court or the Department of Family and Children's Services. Thirty-four (at this writing) trained volunteers are available to supervise visits. The program is actually run in the church, which is located on a seven-acre site. Space available to the program includes five classrooms and a kitchen. In addition, there is a picnic space outside with a large grill. The program operates on Thursdays and Saturdays.

One or two volunteers (usually at least one male) are assigned to each family at a visitation. Volunteers are instructed to "sit, look, and listen." They also record their observations using a form that asks for information about the child's conduct toward the parent, how the parent responds to the child and manages the child's behavior, the attitudes of the participants, and duration of the visit. They also keep a record of missed visits, tardiness, early departures, and the number and ages of children present at the visit.

Following are some of the tools the program uses (see Appendix C):

- **Supervised Visitation Referral Form**

   This simple form is used to record the basic information about participants, reason for the visit, number and duration of visits, who is allowed, and special restrictions.

■ *Rules for Successful Visits*

This sets out a code of behavior around visits, addressing such things as transporting the child (the program does not provide transportation), time issues, and use of substances.

■ *Supervised Visitation Release Form*

The parent signs this form to signify that she understands that abuse or neglect must be reported, has read and understands the rules, and understands other relevant issues.

The Family Visitation Center

The Family Visitation Center in Colorado Springs, Colorado, which opened in 1992, arose as a collaborative effort among the El Paso County Department of Social Services, the El Paso County Commissioners, and Middle Shooks Run Neighborhood Association. The focus of concern was families with children in out-of-home care and a need for supervised visitation. Recognizing the limitations on supervised visitation space and resources at the department, the community sought to meet the need by providing a homelike setting with extended hours (8:00 A.M. through 7:30 P.M., Monday through Saturday), using active community volunteerism. The staff suggests that visits should last at least four hours and occur twice per week.

The Family Visitation Center's goals are to facilitate family relations, help families cope with changing relationships, empower parents, enhance child well-being, teach and reinforce new parenting behaviors, accurately assess parent–child interactions, and help with the transition to reunification or another permanent plan.

The initiative began with the purchase of space, an old Victorian house. This was followed by a period of renovations to create the functional yet warm and homelike environment desired. The new configuration of space included an extra porch, a children's play area, a dining room, a greeting room, a meeting room, several offices, two observation rooms, and a mothers' room. In addition, a well-equipped outside play area was built.

Mothers using the center are able to carry on normal parenting activities in the house—give baths, prepare dinner, play games, do laundry, sit and read, work on toilet training—all under the supervision of a caseworker. Staff members (social workers or trained volunteers) observe parent–child interactions, note strengths and stresses, intervene to foster healthy family dynamics, offer hands-on parenting instruction, teach new styles of discipline, and supervise family meetings.

Tools used by the program include the following (see appendix D):

- **Family Visitation Center Rules**

   This provides rules for arrival, behavior during visits, and other areas to ensure maximal quality of visits.

- **Request for Services**

   This is the referral form used for requesting services of the Family Visitation Center.

- **Child Visitation Plan**

   This form provides basic information about the visitation and supervision needs of the referred parent and child.

Neighborhood Foster Care

This is an initiative of the Casey Family Program in Portland, Oregon, and the State Office for Services to Children and Families in Portland. It includes two sites: one serving Northeast Portland's Jefferson community, which focuses on kinship care; and one serving the Centennial School District community in East Multnomah County, which focuses on keeping sibling groups together. These two programs will be described together except where differences are important to maintain. The program articulates a specific expectation that the principles, tools, and models developed here be transferred to public and private child welfare agencies to promote best practice in general.

Neighborhood Foster Care is not a visitation program as much as a comprehensive program to support successful foster and kinship care. Supporting visitation is part of the service. The program is included here because it demonstrates the value of programmatic context and philosophy that facilitate successful visitation.

The program aims to increase the number of quality foster and kinship homes in its service area, achieve reunification or another form of permanence as soon as possible while meeting the needs of children, reduce length of time in out-of-home care, improve provider satisfaction, decrease placement disruptions, improve birth parents' ability to safely care for their children, and reduce recidivism.

Neighborhood Foster Care truly demonstrates ecological foster care practice. The program aims to keep children in their own neighborhoods, where parent-child contact as well as other ongoing connections are more easily sustainable. The program recruits and supports high-quality neighborhood foster and kinship care families and develops networks of these providers, designed to support relationships among foster, kinship, and birth parents and to work with families in a culturally appropriate manner. In addition, the program mobilizes community resources to help keep these families together. Collaboration is critical, as the program emphasizes the joining of foster and kinship families, caseworkers, and birth families to identify and meet children's needs for safety and attachment.

As stated previously, the program is implemented at two sites. The Jefferson site, focusing on kinship care, is located in a residential drug and alcohol treatment center for women. It houses the administrative offices for the community resource worker, visitation space for birth parents and children, and meeting space for families. The Centennial site, focusing on keeping siblings together, is located at an intermediate school, where a family resource center houses this along with other social service programs for children and families. Space includes administrative offices, visitation rooms, and a conference area.

Both sites use provider networks. Foster parents are clustered into networks of eight to ten foster and kinship families to establish links and provide support. Each network contains a family advocate (caseworker), a community resource worker, a network team leader (may be a foster or kinship parent, who receives extra compensation), and foster or kinship parents (who receive a bonus for attending meetings). Each network meets weekly to discuss case management issues, share information, plan, report progress, and socialize. Decisionmaking is a joint effort, within a philosophy that the people closest to the situation should always have a strong voice.

Neighborhood Foster Care encourages frequent visitation. Within 24 hours of placement, the birth parent and foster or kinship care provider and family advocate meet. Within one week the birth and foster or kinship family will have decided on their future contacts and laid the ground rules for visitation, which may take place at the project sites or in community restaurants, schools, or foster or kinship care homes. Birth parents are also encouraged to attend school functions and appointments with their children. Every child has a concurrent plan, developed with the team, in case reunification is not possible. The program includes significant training for participants—staff, providers, and birth families.

Some of the Neighborhood Foster Care tools that may be useful to other programs include the following (see appendix E):

■ ***Birth Parents: Bridging the Gap of Separation With Their Children, A Continuum of Contact (developed by the Department of Children and Family Services, County of Cuyahoga, Ohio)***

This page lists four progressive levels of activities for birth parents as they support their ongoing relationship with a child in care.

■ ***Foster Parents: Bridging the Gap of Separation Between Children and Their Families, A Continuum of Contact (developed by the Department of Children and Family Services, County of Cuyahoga, Ohio)***

This page lists four progressive levels of activities for foster parents as they support the relationship between birth parents and a child in care.

■ ***Social Workers: Bridging the Gap of Separation Between Children and Their Families, A Continuum of Contact (developed by the Department of Children and Family Services, County of Cuyahoga, Ohio)***

This page lists four progressive levels of activities for social workers as they support the relationship between birth parents and foster parents and a child in care

■ ***Cultural Responsiveness Checklist***

Neighborhood Foster Care is designed to honor children's and families' cultures. This checklist enables staff to check themselves along eight dimensions of responsiveness.

■ ***Visitation Checklist***

This checklist reviews the tasks necessary in preparing for visitation.

California Professional Society on the Abuse of Children

In recognition of the importance of visitation to reunification and to assist with supporting both child safety and rights to visitation, in 1993 (updated in 1997) a multidisciplinary task force of the California Professional Society on the Abuse of Children in Los Angeles County saw the need for guidelines to assist decisionmakers in determining when and under what conditions *monitored visits* should be used when sexual abuse is involved. The introduction to this material states that the guidelines are not to be rigidly adhered to but rather "provide a model of desirable professional practice."

The society developed the following set of useful tools (see Appendix F):

- **General information about monitored visits. This covers the following topics:**

  - important points related to monitored visits;

  - the decision to order therapeutic contacts, eventuating in monitored visits;

  - information required from mental health professionals, child protective services, family court services, and expert panel members to assist in determining when to begin therapeutic contacts;

  - therapy for the parties;

  - decisionmaking process for ordering visitation when there is a prima facie case of sexual abuse in dependency cases (Chart I); and

  - decisionmaking process for ordering visitation when sexual abuse allegations appear reasonably credible in family law cases (Chart II).

Together these provide useful information about visitation in sexual abuse situations. Note that the materials differentiate between therapeutic contact and monitored visits. Therapeutic contact occurs first and involves a mental health worker, child protective services worker, or other person who can actively assist the alleged perpetrator and the child to reengage in a relationship. If these contacts indicate that the perpetrator and child can continue their contact without harm to the child, therapeutic contact gives way to monitored visits, which focus primarily on ensuring child physical and psychological safety through adherence to visitation rules that have been agreed on.

- **Location of Monitoring**

  This simple checklist provides some guidance in choosing the place of the visit, from informal community settings to closely monitored rooms.

- **Guidelines for Visiting Party**

  This provides general guidance as to parental behavior during visits as well as specific guidance when sexual abuse allegations are involved.

- **Suggestions for Visiting Persons**

  This provides a list of ways a parent can maximize visitation, including specific words a parent might use in various situations.

- ***Suggestions for Person Transporting Child to and from Monitored Visits***

   This provides guidance to the parent (such as the custodial parent in a divorce situation) or other person transporting a child.

- ***Suggestions for the Monitor***

   This provides suggestions for the monitor in how to maximize parent–child visits.

- ***Suggestions for Children on Monitored Visits***

   This is not written to or for the child but rather provides suggestions for how to involve the child in planning logistics, how to talk with the child, and how to involve the child in determining content of the visits.

SVN

SVN, formed in 1992, is an association of agencies and individual members who provide supervised visitation services. Membership reflects the various origins of supervised visitation programs, some created in conjunction with the court system, others in response to needs of the child protection system, and others growing out of programs for battered women (Straus et al., 1998). Realizing the rapid pace at which the field of supervised visitation was evolving and the great variety among programs, the SVN was concerned about the lack of any standards for practice. Thus, they began to develop what they have described as guidelines representing good practice. The SVN adopted these Standards and Guidelines for Supervised Visitation Network Practice in 1996. The guidelines are comprehensive, covering such things as types of services offered, security, staffing, intake, termination, and recording (Straus et al., 1998). They are presented as a first step, a work-in-progress, and revisions are currently underway.

Though every standard contains information that might be useful to child welfare workers in planning visits when safety is an issue, we will focus here on the following standards that seem most relevant (see appendix G):

- ***14.(a) Conditions for Participation in the Supervised Visitation Program (Rules)***

   Though some of the rules regarding visitation apply primarily to separation and divorce situations, most are equally applicable to child welfare families when safety is an issue.

■ **15.2 Special Preparation in Cases of Family Violence**

This addresses special precautions staff should take when violence, particularly sexual abuse, is an issue.

■ **17. Interventions during Supervised Visits, Terminating a Supervised Visit**

This standard appears as a paragraph that provides guidance for when to terminate a visit.

■ **20.1 Special Considerations in Situations Involving Family Violence: Child Sexual Abuse**

This standard addresses special training, limitations on contact, when to intervene, honoring a child's claim of abuse, and the need for concurrent therapy when sexual abuse is an issue.

Discussion

The effects that programs and practices such as those described here will have on child welfare visitation in general is unclear, though the potential for influence is great. Several of the initiatives reviewed here specifically articulate an intent to inform practice in general.

Overall, visitation centers seem to be a widely accepted solution (Newton 1997) to maintaining visitation when significant safety concerns are present (e.g., sexual abuse, domestic violence, alcohol and other drug involvement, other high-conflict situations). They readily allow for monitoring and supervision that can provide parent-child contact when it would otherwise be impossible, thus both ensuring child safety and protecting rights to visitation.

Yet, the emphasis on safety should not overshadow the teaching and therapeutic potential of visitation centers and supervised visitation. A controlled, well-equipped environment is ideal for observing, correcting, and providing feedback. Such an environment could benefit visitation even when safety is not an issue, though centers should never replace other settings in the child's natural environment, which are ordinarily the first option for visits. Thus, supervised visitation and centers might be considered to supplement other forms of visitation. In addition, the tools developed through these initiatives—formats for observing parent–child interaction, parent agreements on visitation behavior, recording formats—can be used in many visitation situations.

Despite the innovative practices that supervised visitation and visitation centers are bringing, cautions remain.

■ *Funding*

Visitation centers tend to be small and struggling nonprofit organizations that depend on combinations of grants, fees, donations, and state contracts (Clement, 1998). A survey of providers showed that the annual budgets averaged $100,000 and that the actual cost per visit ranged from $15 to $379, with economics of scale a significant factor (Thoennes & Pearson, 1999). Currently there is modest federal funding through grants, and some states have legislation supporting creating centers but may or may not provide the state funding (Clement, 1998). If centers are to become an important ongoing resource, stable funding must be assured.

■ *Integration with other services*

Thoennes and Pearson (1999) point out that supervised visitation is not a stand-alone service, but rather it must be integrated with other community services.

■ *Treatment versus evidence*

Some center personnel have struggled with the expectation that they provide information that will be used in court to support permanency planning decisionmaking or custody issues. This is an issue especially when they rely on trained volunteers to supervise visits. Although the volunteers may be quite competent to observe, record, and intervene, observation by a professional may be required by the court.

■ *Appropriate use*

Though we have said that center-based visitation and other forms of supervised visitation may be helpful to many families, the reality is that most programs have waiting lists. When staff perceive a program as helpful, they tend to refer as many families as they can, despite more restrictive referral criteria. (This has been a persistent problem for family preservation programs.) Thus, there may be the tendency for less conflictual families to be referred and use services that might better be reserved for high-end cases. This has implications for costs as well as best use of resources.

Practitioners and policymakers are encouraged to follow the development of the programs and practices such as those presented in this chapter and to make their own decisions about how they can use this information to improve visitation in their own jurisdictions. That may be through establishment of new programs, expanding or rethinking current programs, or transferring innovations to enhance practice in general.

In any case, these programs and practices are pushing the envelope on our thinking about visitation, underscoring the importance of parent-child contact regardless of the obstacles (such as child safety concerns), stretching our concept of what visitation can and should achieve, and offering some tools for consideration.

References

Barbell, K., & Wright, L. (1999). Introduction: Family foster care in the next century. *Child Welfare, 78*, 3–14.

Bank, S. P., & Kahn, M. D. (1982). *The sibling bond.* New York: Basic Books.

Beckerman, A. (1998). Charting a course: Meeting the challenge of permanency planning for children with incarcerated mothers. *Child Welfare, 77*, 513–529.

Benedict, M. I., Zuravin, S., & Stallings, R. Y. (1996). Adult functioning of children who lived in kin versus non-relative family foster homes. *Child Welfare, 75*, 529–549.

Berrick, J. D. (1997). Assessing quality of care in kinship and foster family care. *Family Relations, 46*, 273–280.

Beyer, M. (1999a). Parent-child visits as an opportunity for change. *Prevention Report,* 2–10. National Resource Center for Family Centered Practice.

Beyer, M. (1999b). Parent-child visits as an opportunity for change: Visit principles. *Prevention Report,* 11–12. National Resource Center for Family Centered Practice.

Bloom, B. (1995). Imprisoned mothers. In K. Gabel & Johnson (Eds.), *Children of incarcerated parents* (pp. 21–30). New York: Lexington Books.

Bowlby, J. (1969). *Attachment and loss: Vol. I. Attachment.* New York: Basic Books.

Cantos, A. L., Gries, L. T., & Slis, V. (1997). Behavioral correlates of parental visiting during family foster care. *Child Welfare, 76*, 309–329.

Casey Family Program. (n.d.). *Neighborhood foster care guidebook.* Portland, OR: Author.

Cestero, J. M. (1997). Happiness is being a grandparent? The evolution of grandparent visitation in Florida. *Florida Bar Journal, 71*(10), 51–53.

Chiancone, J. (1997). Visitation: What lawyers should know. *Child Law Practice, 16*(6), 85–89.

Child Welfare League of America. (1995). *CWLA standards of excellence for family foster care services* (Rev. ed.). Washington, DC: Author.

Child Welfare League of America. (2000). *CWLA standards of excellence for kinship care services.* Washington, DC: Author.

Clement, D.A. (1998). A compelling need for mandated use of supervised visitation programs. *Family and Conciliation Courts Review, 36*(2), 294–316.

Clemons, R. (1999). *Visitation survey: Executive summary.* Erie, PA: Department of Human Services, Office of Children and Youth.

Courtney, M. E. (1996). Kinship foster care and children's welfare: The California experience. *Focus, 17*(3), 42–48.

Davis, I. P., Landsverk, J., Newton, R., & Ganger, W. (1996). Parental visiting and foster care reunification. *Children and Youth Services Review, 18*(4/5), 363–382.

Egan, N.F. (n.d.). *People potential* [Transparencies]. For National Resource Center for Permanency Planning and The Families Together Project of St. Christopher.

Falberg, V. (1979). *Attachment and separation: Putting the pieces together.* Evergreen, CO: Forest Heights Lodge.

Faller, K. C. (1993). *Child sexual abuse: Intervention and treatment issues.* Washington, DC: National Center on Child Abuse and Neglect.

Gleeson, J. P., O'Donnell, J., & Bonecutter, F. J. (1997). Understanding the complexity of practice in kinship foster care. *Child Welfare, 76,* 801–826.

Hairston, C. F. (1998). The forgotten parent: Understanding the factors that influence incarcerated fathers' relationships with their children. *Child Welfare, 77,* 617–639.

Hartfield, B. W. (1996). Legal recognition of the value of intergenerational nurturance: Grandparent visitation statutes in the nineties. *Generations, 20*(1), 53–56.

Henrique, Z. M. (1982). *Imprisoned mothers and their children.* Washington, DC: University Press of America.

Hess, P. (1999). (Ed.). *Enhancing visiting services: Standards, leadership, organization, and collaboration.* Philadelphia: Commonwealth of Pennsylvania Department of Public Welfare.

Hess, P. (1988). Case and context: Determinants of planned visit frequency in foster family care. *Child Welfare, 68,* 311–326.

Hess, P., & Proch, K. (1993). Visiting: The heart of reunification. In B. Pine, R. Warsh, & A. Maluccio (Eds.), *Together again: Family reunification in foster care.* Washington, DC: Child Welfare League of America.

Hess, P., & Proch, K. (1988). *Family visiting of children in out-of-home care: A practical guide.* Washington, DC: Child Welfare League of America.

Hewitt, S. (1991). Therapeutic management of preschool cases of alleged but unsubstantiated sexual abuse. *Child Welfare, 70,* 59–67.

Horejsi, C., Bertsche, A., & Clark, F. (1981). *Social work practice with parents of children in foster care.* Springfield, IL: Charles Thomas.

Jackson, S. M. (1996). The kinship triad: A service delivery model. *Child Welfare, 75,* 583–599.

Jenkins, S., & Norman, E. (1972). *Filial deprivation and foster care.* New York: Columbia University Press.

Katz, P. (1998). Supporting families and children of mothers in jail: An integrated child welfare and criminal justice strategy. *Child Welfare, 77,* 495–511.

Lee, R. E., & Lynche, M. T. (1998). Combating foster care drift: An ecosystemic treatment model for neglect cases. *Contemporary Family Therapy, 20*(3), 351–370.

Link, M. K. (1996). Permanency outcomes in kinship care: Astudy of children placed in kinship care in Erie County, New York. *Child Welfare, 75,* 509–528.

Littner, N. (1975). The importance of natural parents to the child in placement. *Child Welfare 54,* 175–181.

Loar, L. (1998). Making visits work. *Child Welfare, 77,* 41–57.

McLean, B., & Thomas, R. (1996). Informal and formal kinship care populations: Study in contrasts. *Child Welfare, 75,* 489–505.

Melina, L. R., & Roszia, S. K. (1993). *The open adoption experience.* New York: HarperPerrenial.

Millham, S., Bullock, R., Hosie, K., & Haak, M. (1986). *Lost in care: The problems of maintaining links between children in care and their families.* Aldershot, Hampshire, UK: Gower Publishing Company.

Mills, C. S., & Usher, D. (1996). A kinship care case management approach. *Child Welfare, 75,* 599–618.

Newton, B. S. (1997). Visitation centers: A solution without critics. *Florida Bar Journal, 71*(1), 54–57.

Oppenheim, E., & Bussiere, A. (1996). Adoption: Where do relatives stand? *Child Welfare, 75,* 471–489.

Oysterman, D., & Benbenishty, R. (1992). Keeping in touch: Ecological factors related to foster care visitation. *Child and Adolescent Social Work Journal, 9,* 541–554.

Proch, K., & Howard, J.A. (1986). Parental visiting of children in foster care. *Social Work, 31*(3), 178–181.

Schafran, L. H., Wu, Y., Bulkley, J., & Sandt, C. (1996). *Adjudicating allegations of child sexual abuse when custody is in dispute.* New York: National Education Program to Promote Equality for Women and Men in the Courts.

Seymour, C., & Hairston, C. F. (1998). Children with parents in prison: Child welfare policy, program, and practice issues. *Child Welfare, 77,* 469–491.

Simms, M. D., & Bolden, B. J. (1991). The family reunification project: Facilitating regular contact among foster children biological families, and foster families. *Child Welfare, 70,* 679–690.

Snell, T. S., & Morton, D. C. (1994). *Bureau of justice special report: Women in prison* (NCJ-145321). Washington, DC: U.S. Department of Justice, Office of Justice Programs, Bureau of Justice Statistics.

Straus, R. B., Blaschak-Brown, N., & Reinger, A. (1998). Standards and guidelines for Supervised Visitation Network practice: An introductory discussion. *Family and Conciliation Courts Review, 36*(1), 96–107.

Thoennes, N., & Pearson, J. (1999). Supervised visitation: A profile of providers. *Family and Conciliation Courts Review, 37*(4), 460–477.

Tortorella, M. (1996). When supervised visitation is in the best interests of the child. *Family Law Quarterly, 30*(1), 199–215.

Wallerstein, J. S., & Kelly, J. B. (1980). *Surviving the breakup: How children and parents cope with divorce.* New York: Basic Books.

Warsh, R., Maluccio, A., & Pine B. (1994). *Teaching family reunification: A sourcebook.* Washington, DC: Child Welfare League of America.

Women's Prison Association. (1996). *When a mother is arrested: How the criminal justice and child welfare systems can work together more effectively.* Baltimore: Maryland Department of Human Resources.

Wright, L., & Seymour, C. (2000). *Working with children and families separated by incarceration.* Washington, DC: Child Welfare League of America.

Appendix A

The tools presented in this appendix are summaries of information provided in the chapters of this publication. They are not meant to be used apart from the fuller understandings of visitation that this text provides, but rather they are intended as simplified reminders that can be used by child welfare professionals as well as others involved in visitation to guide their thinking

Benefits of Visitation

To ensure that you are getting full benefits from visitation, check against this list.

- Ease the pain of separation and loss for all.

- Maintain and strengthen family relationships.

- Reassure the child of parent's well-being.

- Deal with changing relationships and support family in coping with changes.

- Enhance parental motivation to change through providing reassurance and hope.

- Enhance parental empowerment.

- Provide the opportunity for parental change.

- Help participants deal with reality.

- Support the child's adjustment in the foster home.

- Provide the context for self-assessment and agency assessment.

- Support decisionmaking.

- Reduce time in care.

- Increase the likelihood of reunification.

- Assist with transition to reunification.

- Contribute to family stability once reunification has occurred.

- Provide the forum for ongoing information sharing.

- Enable the parent to stay current with the child's development and activities.

- Support child developmental progression.

- If reunification is not the plan, help participants cope with another plan, grieve, work out their future relationship.

- Provide the material needed for accurate, verifiable documentation.

Summary of ASFA Provisions in
Relation to Visitation

Use this table to review ASFA provisions and to ensure that you are carrying out visitation in accordance with the implications of ASFA.

ASFA Provision/Focus	Implications for Visitation
Safety is the paramount concern	Visitation should be used both to help parents learn safe parenting practices and to incrementally test their ability to safely parent.
Emphasizes reasonable efforts and identifies circumstances when reasonable efforts are not required	Ensuring that visitation occurs and providing supports for visitation is included in reasonable efforts; lack of support for visitation makes the agency vulnerable in seeking termination of parental rights. The decision to bypass reasonable efforts (including visitation support) requires careful documentation.
Reduced time frames for first permanency hearing (12 months rather than 18 months)	Visitation should begin immediately with the permanency goal clearly the focus.
Begin TPR proceedings for children who have been in care for 15 of the last 22 months (unless child is with relatives or there is a compelling reason not to TPR, or the family has not received services)	Visitation should begin immediately with the permanency goal clearly the focus; visitation should provide clear evidence that TPR is or is not in the child's best interest; visitation is a most important service that must be provided for the family in terms of reasonable efforts unless it is clearly precluded; use visitation to support TPR and the adoption permanency option.
Concurrent planning option	In response to reduced time frames, concurrent planning (for reunification and some other permanency option) is an important service; visitation is the tool for full disclosure and for testing permanency options.
Emphasis on kinship care	Though a child may be in kinship care, this does not reduce the need for visitation and does not change the purposes of visitation, though there will be special considerations around visitation in relation to kinship care.
Recognition of substance abuse as a significant child welfare issue	Consider special concerns around visitation when substances are involved; consider use of supervised visitation as well as special programs.
Focus on results and accountability; procedural safeguard no longer sufficient	Results include not only safety and permanence but also well-being, suggesting that services, including visitation, must consider the health and development of children in care.
Innovative approaches emphasized	Given the importance of visitation, agencies should be proactive in finding new ways to ensure that it occurs and is effective at meeting its designed purposes.

Guide to Planning for Visitation

This matrix can be used to review the variety of decisions that must be made in planning for visitation.

VARIABLES/ DIMENSIONS	OVERRIDING ISSUES/FACTORS					
	Safety	Permanency Goal	Stages, Time in Care	Family, Culture	Age of Child	Handling Logistics
Timing: • how soon • how often • duration						
Place: • child's home • foster home • agency • center • natural environment • professional appointment						
Participants: • father • siblings, pets • other relatives • friends • professionals						
Content: • attachment • parenting • child development • decisionmaking						
Controls: • secure place • observation • supervision • rules						

Whom to Involve in Visitation

Answering these questions will help the worker and others decide who should be involved in visitation.

- Who do parent and child suggest should be involved?

- What part (if any) did the person play in the maltreatment (particularly where sexual or severe physical abuse is involved), and can the child be adequately protected?

- What positive role did the person play in the child's life?

- What positive role might the person play in the child's current and future life?

- Overall, how can visitation with this person contribute toward achievement of the permanency goal?

- Does the child for any reason veto visits that include this person?

Confidentiality

Here are some suggestions concerning handling confidentiality issues around visitation.

- Discuss confidentiality openly with parent and child
  - Explain to them the concept of confidentiality.
  - Explain the limits of confidentiality.
  - Help them weigh the benefits versus the harm of including certain participants in visitation, in light of possible breaches of confidentiality.
  - Have them identify any topics that are particularly sensitive and that they would like protected.
  - Have them help you draft guidelines around confidentiality for their visits.
  - Give them veto power over inclusion of participants.

- Discuss confidentiality openly with all participants, ensuring their understanding and gaining their concurrence.
  - Explain confidentiality in concrete behaviors to ensure that they understand what it means.
  - Explain the unpleasant consequences for parent and child when confidentiality is broken.
  - Distribute and discuss guidelines drafted with the parent and child.

- When breaches of confidentiality occur, handle this openly.
  - Explore why it happened to see if it can be avoided in the future.
  - Make it clear the harm that was done by the breach, with the offended party specifically stating feelings or other repercussions.
  - Have the team decide if the offending party should discontinue involvement with visitation, with the offended person having a major voice.

Principles of Visitation

The following principles guide practice in relation to visitation. The list can be used to check that all decisions around visitation are consistent with these principles.

- Visitation is sacrosanct.

- Decisions and conclusions based upon participant behaviors in relation to visitation must reflect a deep understanding of the emotional impact of separation and visitation and deep empathy for all participants.

- Visitation is a collaborative venture, inclusive in the broadest sense.

- Discussions around visitation should be characterized by openness and full disclosure of any relevant information.

- Visitation needs support.

- Visitation planning should include an ecological perspective.

- Visitation planning is not static.

- Risk is an ever-present consideration, but there is almost always a way to control for risk without discontinuing visits.

- The core question in planning visitation is how decisions around particular variables support the purposes of visitation for a particular family and child.

- Use visitation to support family ties, regardless of the permanency goal.

The First Visit

Use this list to check that you have prepared well for the first visit and conducted appropriate follow-up. It can also be used (modified) for subsequent visits.

- At the point of separation talk about the first visit.

- If visitation is addressed in the court order, use that as the basis for early planning.

- Determine if the visit needs to be supervised or needs other restrictions.

- Decide who needs to be present at the first visit.

- Decide on the place for the visit.

- Arrange and coordinate transportation, child care, or other logistics to support visitation.

- Tend to the purpose of the visit.

- Write it down.

- Distribute the plan to primary participants.

- Prepare all participants in terms of what will occur during the visit.

- Prepare all participants in terms of emotional readiness.

- Coach, rehearse, and troubleshoot.

- Provide reassurance that you will be available after the visit to help the participant with any questions or issues in relation to the visit.

- Be available at the time of the visit.

- Follow through with your promise of availability after the visit.

- Document.

Managing Ongoing Emotions

Use this list to ensure that you have dealt with participants' emotions during all stages of visitation.

- Prepare all participants before the first visit.
- Set behavioral expectations.
- Help everyone focus on the needs of the child.
- Respect the child's emotions as you would any other participant's.
- Be attentive and responsive to the child's ongoing postvisit reactions.
- Be attentive and responsive to the parent's ongoing reactions to visitation.
- Deal with emotions during visits.
- Deal with reactions around reunification.
- Deal with reactions around changing the plan.
- Deal with your own and other participants' reactions.

Philosophy of Parenting

This list may be used to review your own approach to teaching parenting and to help parents themselves make sense out of parenting and integrate what they are learning.

- Parenting is about relationship. (Preserve it.)
- Parenting is ongoing conflict resolution. (Expect it, solve it.)
- Parenting involves mutual influencing and growing. (Be open to it.)
- Parenting builds discipline in parents as well as in children. (Treasure it.)
- Parenting, because it involves growth, also involves pain. (Tolerate it.)
- Parenting is about building rather than tearing down. (Enjoy it. Enjoy people-making.)
- Parenting is for the long term. (Focus on it. Win the war.)
- Parenting is ongoing self-assessment. (Learn it.)
- Parenting is being. (Become it.)

Teaching Parenting

The parent needs to master the following steps that lead to positive interactions with a child. In assessing parenting ability and designing an intervention, the worker and/or team will want to consider parental strengths and deficits in each of these areas.

- Understanding that there is a relationship between what the parent does and child behavior and development.
- Paying attention to cues.
- Interpreting cues.
- Responding appropriately.
- Learning from interaction cycles.

Techniques for Teaching Parenting

To fully take advantage of the opportunities to teach parenting, workers should check that they are including the following:

- Coach and rehearse the parent before the visit.
- Plan parent–child interactions that specifically support parenting skills.
- Plan parent–child interactions that specifically support relationship and family connection.
- Plan parent–child interactions that support child development.
- Coach and model appropriate parenting behaviors during the visit.
- Critique after the visit, using videotapes of the session or participants' memories of the visit. The critique should

  - communicate appreciation of the parent's expertise in knowing her own child,
  - communicate appreciation of the parent's individuality,
  - reinforce positives and avoid negative references,
  - offer suggestions in a manner that communicates common exploration of approaches and techniques rather than criticism and correction, and
  - connect to the principles of parenting discussed earlier.

Appendix B

**Tools from the
Catholic Charities
Therapeutic Supervised
Visitation Program**

CATHOLIC CHARITIES OF BUFFALO, N.Y.
THERAPEUTIC SUPERVISED VISITATION AGREEMENT
POLICY AGREEMENT

PLEASE CHECK EACH ITEM AS YOU REVIEW THE FOLLOWING VISITATION POINTS.

_____ I will not use drugs or alcohol before visiting with my child(ren). I understand that my visit may be cancelled if there is a suspicion that these substances have been used.

_____ I will arrive at Catholic Charities Therapeutic Supervised Visitation at the specified time of arrival 15 minutes before visit is to begin and leave 15 minutes after the visit has ended.

_____ I will ask for prior approval from the Visitation Therapist and/or any other deemed authority before bringing someone else to the visit.

_____ I will not bring any weapons or articles that could be used as a weapon to visits. I understand that Catholic Charities Therapeutic Visitation security officer has the right to search for weapons and, if necessary, check in on visits.

_____ I will not follow or harass another party before, during or after a scheduled visit.

_____ I will not speak negatively about the child(ren)'s custodial parent or foster parent in front of the child(ren).

_____ I will not talk about adult issues, such as court proceedings, with the child(ren).

_____ I will not make promises to the children about future living arrangements or unsupervised visits.

_____ I will not question the child(ren) about their custodial parent's or foster parent's whereabouts or activities.

_____ I will not send any correspondence (i.e. regarding child support) or messages to the custodial or foster parent by means of the child(ren).

_____ I will not use physical punishment or threaten to use physical punishment with the child(ren) during visits.

_____ If the child (ren) makes make any statement or reference to any alleged or confirmed abuse I will not deny the child(ren)'s statement and will listen to what the child(ren) say.

_____ I will follow the suggestions of the Visitation Therapist and their assistants while visiting the child(ren).

_____ I will notify the Visitation Therapist as soon as possible if I cannot attend a visit.

_____ I understand that breaking this agreement may lead to the termination of visitation at Catholic Charities.

_____ I understand that it is Visitation Therapist's responsibility to report to the ECDSS, and or any representative of the Court of any circumstance that relates to my ability to parent my children in a safe and positive manner.

_____ I understand that written Observation Reports will be sent to _____.

_____ I have received a copy of these policies.

_____   _____
Signature of Visiting Parent   **Date**

_____   _____
Visitation Therapist   **Date**

OBSERVATION FORM *

CATHOLIC CHARITIES OF BUFFALO, N.Y.
VISITATION PROGRAMS
1581 Bailey Avenue
Buffalo, NY 14212
896-6390

Date of Visit: _____

CASE NAME: _____ Date Form Completed: _____

LOG #: _____ Visit Number: _____

Visitation Therapist / Aide: _____

Case Planner / Law Guardian: _____

Visiting Adult(s)   Visiting Child(ren)

_____   _____
_____   _____
_____   _____
_____   _____
_____   _____

Visiting Adult(s) on time?   _____ Yes   _____ No

Visit Started: _____ am / pm   Visit Ended: _____ am / pm

Time / Attendance Concerns: _____

_____

_____

I. INITIAL CONTACTS

   A. Greeting Between Child(ren) and Visiting Adult(s)
       _____ Hug _____ Kiss _____ Verbal Greeting Only

   B. Initiated By:
       ____ Adult(s) ____ Child(ren) ____ Mutual ____ Direct Greeting Avoided by Child(ren)

   Comments: _____

   _____

CASE NAME: _____   CASE PLANNER: _____

VISITATION GOALS

Please check category of goals being addressed

_____ **SAFETY**

_____ **PARENT(S)' RESPONSE TO CHILD'S NEEDS**

_____ **ATTACHMENT / BONDING**

_____ **PARENT SKILLS** (circle)

Physical Care   Structure   Positive Reinforcement of Desired Behaviors   Discipline

_____ **COMMUNICATION SKILLS** (circle)

Language of Feelings   Talking Feelings (Parent/Child)   Listening to Feelings (Parent/Child)

Sharing Life Events (Parent/Child)   Listening to Life Events (Parent/Child)

_____ **HEALING** (circle)

Separation Trauma   Past Alleged Physical Abuse   Past Alleged Sexual Abuse   Neglect   Domestic Violence

_____ **OTHER, Specify:** _____

_____

IMMEDIATE GOALS FOR THIS SESSION ARE:

1. _____

_____

2. _____

_____

ACTIVITIES/INTERVENTIONS USED TO ACHIEVE GOALS BY PARENT, CHILD, &/OR THERAPIST:

_____

_____

_____

_____

_____

ACCOMPLISHMENTS: _____

_____

_____

_____

NEEDS WORK: _____

_____

_____

_____

PLAN FOR NEXT SESSION: _____

_____

_____

_____

CASE NAME: _____ CASE PLANNER: _____

II. GENERAL VISIT ACTIVITIES

_____ Selected from those available at Center
_____ Brought by child(ren), visiting adult(s)

Comments: _____

_____

_____

_____

III. CHILD(REN)'S MOOD AND BEHAVIOR DURING VISIT

_____

withdrawn / relaxed / fidgeting / verbal aggression / physical aggression
(Place an **X** , or the child(ren)'s name(s) in the area which best describes behavior during visit.)

Comments: _____

_____

_____

_____

_____

IV. THERAPIST INTERVENTION

____ Facilitating Activities ____ Interrupting Parental Behavior ____ Taking Child Out of Room

Explain: _____

_____

_____

_____

_____

V. VISIT ENDING

A. Separation of Visiting Parties
___ Hug ___ Kiss ___Verbal Only ___ Stated "I love you" ___ Resisted Overtures for Hug/Kiss

B. Initiated By:
_____ Therapist _____ Parent _____ Child _____ Mutual (Parent & Child)

C. Other:
_____ Adult delays visit's end _____ Child(ren) leaves room prior to visit's end
_____ Child(ren) delay visit's end _____ Visit ended by Visitation Therapist

Comments: _____

_____

_____

```
┌─────────────────────────────────────────────────────────┐
│                  CATHOLIC CHARITIES                       │
│        VISITATION  PERFORMANCE  OUTCOME  SCALE            │
└─────────────────────────────────────────────────────────┘
```

__Please Circle Program__

Therapeutic Supervised Visitation   **Therapeutic Parent / Child Access**

Goals / Outcome Scale

Visiting Parent: _____   Date of 1st Visit: _____

Visitation Therapist: _____   Date of 1st Assessment: _____
2nd Observer/Volunteer _____

Number of Children: _____   Date of 2nd Assessment: _____

Termination Assessment Date: _____   Date of 3rd Assessment: _____

Instructions: Please complete the 1st Assessment within the initial 3 visits, after 15 visits, after 45 visits, and at termination. Enter the "Skill Point Score" in the space below. Using a __red__ pencil, color in the performance percentage for each of the skill areas.

SKILL POINT SCORE = [   ] out of a possible [   ]   **TOTAL PERCENT**
                    Sum of answered items   Ideal Score

PARENT SKILL AREAS

Performance Outcomes

%

100					
90					
80					
70					
60					
50					
40					
30					
20					
10					
0					

I. Attachment   II. Parent   III. Communication   IV. Parent's Response   V. Healing
   Bonding   Skills   to Child's Needs

Percentage

_____   _____   _____   _____   _____
   I   II   III   IV   V

RATING SCALE KEY
NA = Not Applicable, not observed
0 = Does not have or use the skill
1 = Uses the skill only with assistance
2 = Uses the skill only with frequent intervention
3 = Uses the skill with minimal intervention
4 = Uses the skill independently

I. ATTACHMENT /BONDING

1. Parent consistently attends scheduled visits.   NA 0 1 2 3 4

2. Parent discusses missed visits honestly with child(ren).   NA 0 1 2 3 4

Infant Attachment/Bonding (0 - 2 years*)

3. Parent initiates behaviors that promote attachment and bonding.   NA 0 1 2 3 4

4. Parent positions infant for reciprocal exchange, talks and/or sings to, and rocks infants.   NA 0 1 2 3 4

5. Parent identifies infant's cues for hunger, wet or soiled.   NA 0 1 2 3 4

6. Parent responds to infant's cues for attention.   NA 0 1 2 3 4

7. Parent shows pleasure towards infant in gaze, voice or smile.   NA 0 1 2 3 4

8. Parent makes positive remarks to infant.   NA 0 1 2 3 4

9. Parent engages in pleasureable give an take with infant during play.   NA 0 1 2 3 4

Toddler Attachment/bonding (2 - 4 years)

10. Parent initiates behaviors that promote toddler attachment and bonding.   NA 0 1 2 3 4

11. Parent identifies toddler's cues of hunger, wet or soiled.   NA 0 1 2 3 4

12. Parent responds to toddler's cues for attention.   NA 0 1 2 3 4

13. Parent engages in play with toddler, e.g., plays pat-a-cake, counting eyes, ears, teeth, etc., "Eensie Weensie Spider", "Thumpkin", etc.   NA 0 1 2 3 4

14. Parent initiates language, uses child's name frequently, etc.   NA 0 1 2 3 4

Pre-School Age Attachment/Bonding (4 - 6 years)

15. Parent initiates behaviors that promote attachment and bonding with pre-school age child.   NA 0 1 2 3 4

*These are suggested chronological ages, please also consider developmental stages and differences.

RATING SCALE KEY
NA = Not Applicable, not observed
0 = Does not have or use the skill
1 = Uses the skill only with assistance
2 = Uses the skill only with frequent intervention
3 = Uses the skill with minimal intervention
4 = Uses the skill independently

16. Parent initiates activities and games that are shared, e.g.,
"Simon Says", "Hide and Find blocks", Block building,
Puzzles, Drawings, etc.   NA 0 1 2 3 4

17. Parent responds appropriately to child's questions including
those regarding foster parents, and those that are about
parent, history, etc.   NA 0 1 2 3 4

18. Parent identifies child's cues for closeness/distance, physical
and emotional needs, and responds appropriately.   NA 0 1 2 3 4

19. Parent's affect matches messages being given to child.   NA 0 1 2 3 4

Latency Age Attachment/bonding (7 - 11 years)

20. Parent initiates behaviors that promote attachment and
bonding with Latency age child.   NA 0 1 2 3 4

21. Parent initiates activities and games that are shared and
encourages talking, e.g., board games, photo albums, etc.   NA 0 1 2 3 4

22. Parent encourages discussion of such topics as fears, likes/
dislikes, street dangers, peer relationships, etc.   NA 0 1 2 3 4

23. Parent responds appropriately to child's cues for closeness/
distance, physical and emotional needs.   NA 0 1 2 3 4

24. Parent's affect matches messages being given.   NA 0 1 2 3 4

25. Parent responds honestly and appropriately to questions
regarding history, foster parents, etc.   NA 0 1 2 3 4

Adolescent Attachment/Bonding (12 - 18 years)

26. Parent initiates behaviors that promote attachment and
bonding with Adolesent age child.   NA 0 1 2 3 4

27. Parent initiates activities that match the needs and interest
of child.   NA 0 1 2 3 4

28. Parent negotiates with child when differences emerge, e.g.,
board games, cards, checkers, etc.   NA 0 1 2 3 4

RATING SCALE KEY
NA = Not Applicable, not observed
0 = Does not have or use the skill
1 = Uses the skill only with assistance
2 = Uses the skill only with frequent intervention
3 = Uses the skill with minimal intervention
4 = Uses the skill independently

29. Parent encourages discussion of such topics as history, peer relationships, school, family, etc.

NA 0 1 2 3 4

30. Parent responds appropriately to child's cues for closeness/distance, physical and emotional needs.

NA 0 1 2 3 4

31. Parent's affect matches messages given.

NA 0 1 2 3 4

SUMMARY OF ATTACHMENT/BONDING GOALS

Sum of answered items = _____ "Total Score"
# of Answered items _____ x 4 = _____ "Ideal Score"

Total Score [ ] _____ = _____ % Ideal Score [ ]

Comments:_____

_____

_____

_____

II. PARENT SKILLS

Physical Care (Infants)

1. Parent feeds infant whenever necessary.

NA 0 1 2 3 4

2. Parent recognizes infant's cry and responds immediately.

NA 0 1 2 3 4

3. Parent holds infant in semi-upright position while feeding.

NA 0 1 2 3 4

4. Parent feeds bottle or food until infant no longer takes bottle or is gone, burps infant.

NA 0 1 2 3 4

5. Parent changes infant's diapers whenever necessary.

NA 0 1 2 3 4

6. Parent recognizes infant's cry of being wet or soiled.

NA 0 1 2 3 4

7. Parent checks diaper and secures infant on changing table.

NA 0 1 2 3 4

8. Parent physically removes and discards diaper.

NA 0 1 2 3 4

9. Parent cleans infant, secures a clean diaper, and re-clothes infant.

NA 0 1 2 3 4

RATING SCALE KEY
NA = Not Applicable, not observed
0 = Does not have or use the skill
1 = Uses the skill only with assistance
2 = Uses the skill only with frequent intervention
3 = Uses the skill with minimal intervention
4 = Uses the skill independently

Physical Care (Toddlers)

10.	Parent responds to child's cues.	NA 0 1 2 3 4
11.	Parent notices child's cues of hunger and feeds.	NA 0 1 2 3 4
12.	Parent notices child's cues of fatigue and soothes.	NA 0 1 2 3 4
13.	Parent notices child's cues of being hurt and cares appropriately for child.	NA 0 1 2 3 4

Structure

14.	Parent plans activities and allots time frames for each activity.	NA 0 1 2 3 4
15.	Parent selects age appropriate activities e.g., games, coloring, etc.	NA 0 1 2 3 4
16.	Parent reviews these activities in pre-visit.	NA 0 1 2 3 4
17.	Parent participates in activities during visit.	NA 0 1 2 3 4
18.	Parent plans and executes the development of a family rules chart with the child.	NA 0 1 2 3 4
19.	Parent uses positive reinforcement with child.	NA 0 1 2 3 4
20.	Parent identifies positive behaviors to be supported.	NA 0 1 2 3 4
21.	Parent makes statements e.g., "you're doing a great job, "thank you:, "please", etc.	NA 0 1 2 3 4
22.	Parent rewards good behaior with material objects when warranted.	NA 0 1 2 3 4
23.	Parent utilizes a range of behaviors to extinguish negative behaviors.	NA 0 1 2 3 4
24.	Parent ignores unwanted behaviors when appropriate.	NA 0 1 2 3 4
25.	Parent warns child prior to placing child in "time-out".	NA 0 1 2 3 4
26.	Parent uses an appropriate time limit depending on age of child and announces to child.	NA 0 1 2 3 4

RATING SCALE KEY
NA = Not Applicable, not observed
0 = Does not have or use the skill
1 = Uses the skill only with assistance
2 = Uses the skill only with frequent intervention
3 = Uses the skill with minimal intervention
4 = Uses the skill independently

27.   Parent selects a spot apart from rest of visiting children.   NA 0 1 2 3 4

28.   Parent ignores the child during "time-out".   NA 0 1 2 3 4

29.   Parent invites child back to group when time-out is over.   NA 0 1 2 3 4

SUMMARY OF PARENT SKILLS GOALS

Sum of answered items = _____ "Total Score"
# of Answered items _____ x 4 = _____ "Ideal Score"

Total Score [   ]   _____ = _____ %   Ideal Score [   ]

Comments: _____
_____
_____
_____

III. COMMUNICATION

1.   Parent introduces the language of feelings into visits.   NA 0 1 2 3 4

2.   Parent uses feeling words and helps child understand their
      meaning.   NA 0 1 2 3 4

3.   Parent helps child understand their feelings by noticing
      and labeling them in the visit.   NA 0 1 2 3 4

4.   Parent helps child understand different feelings through
      activities such as reading, watching videos, using feeling   NA 0 1 2 3 4
      faces and drawing.

5.   Parent models how to share feelings by talking to child about
      his/her own feelings.   NA 0 1 2 3 4

6.   Parent makes eye contact, asks questions of the child to make
      sure child understands the feeling shared.   NA 0 1 2 3 4

7.   Parent listens to child's expression of feelings.   NA 0 1 2 3 4

8.   Parent uses play activities that help child share feelings.   NA 0 1 2 3 4

9.   Parent makes eye contact, shows interest in what child is
      saying through body language and facial expression.   NA 0 1 2 3 4

RATING SCALE KEY
NA = Not Applicable, not observed
0 = Does not have or use the skill
1 = Uses the skill only with assistance
2 = Uses the skill only with frequent intervention
3 = Uses the skill with minimal intervention
4 = Uses the skill independently

10.	Parent listens to child without interrupting.	NA 0 1 2 3 4
11.	Parent encourages child to share more by asking questions and validating child's feelings.	NA 0 1 2 3 4
12.	Parent participates in activities with child that facilitate the sharing of life events.	NA 0 1 2 3 4
13.	Parent makes eye contact, matches appropriate facial expression with life event shared.	NA 0 1 2 3 4
14.	Parent talks to child about his/her recent activities and other family members.	NA 0 1 2 3 4
15.	Parent talks to child about memories of past shared activities between parent & child.	NA 0 1 2 3 4
16.	Parent facilitates their child's sharing of life events.	NA 0 1 2 3 4
17.	Parent makes eye contact while listening.	NA 0 1 2 3 4
18.	Parent avoids interrupting the child, and exhibits interest in what child is saying through body language and facial expression.	NA 0 1 2 3 4
19.	Parent responds with appropriate feeling and validation of life event shared.	NA 0 1 2 3 4
20.	Parent asks questions about life events to encourage more in depth conversation about event.	NA 0 1 2 3 4

SUMMARY OF COMMUNICATION GOALS

Sum of answered items = _____ "Total Score"
# of Answered items _____ x 4 = _____ "Ideal Score"

Total Score [ ] _____ = _____ %   Ideal Score [ ]

Comments:_____
_____
_____
_____

RATING SCALE KEY
NA = Not Applicable, not observed
0 = Does not have or use the skill
1 = Uses the skill only with assistance
2 = Uses the skill only with frequent intervention
3 = Uses the skill with minimal intervention
4 = Uses the skill independently

IV. PARENT'S RESPONSE TO CHILD'S NEEDS

1. Parent separates their needs from those of their child. NA 0 1 2 3 4

2. Parent differentiates their feelings, e.g., scared, angry, hungry, tired, etc., from those of their child. NA 0 1 2 3 4

3. Parent puts aside their own feelings and responds to child's feelings. NA 0 1 2 3 4

4. Parent understands their appropriate roles and responsibilities as a parent. NA 0 1 2 3 4

5. Parent takes initiative in engaging child in focused activities, conversation, etc. NA 0 1 2 3 4

6. Parent takes responsibility for outcome of visit and goal achievement or lack or achievement. NA 0 1 2 3 4

SUMMARY OF PARENT RESPONSE TO CHILD'S NEEDS GOALS

Sum of answered items = _____ "Total Score"
# of Answered items _____ x 4 = _____ "Ideal Score"

Total Score [ ] _____ = _____ %   Ideal Score [ ]

Comments:_____
_____
_____
_____

V. HEALING

Infant/Toddler (Pre-Verbal)

1. Parent recognizes and manages child's trauma responses, e.g., crying, tantrums, refusing to leave visit room, etc. NA 0 1 2 3 4

All Age Children

2. Parent accepts that trauma has occurred to child (e.g., separation, abuse, exposure to violence, etc.) NA 0 1 2 3 4

3. Parent initiates conversation about trauma. NA 0 1 2 3 4

RATING SCALE KEY
NA = Not Applicable, not observed
0 = Does not have or use the skill
1 = Uses the skill only with assistance
2 = Uses the skill only with frequent intervention
3 = Uses the skill with minimal intervention
4 = Uses the skill independently

4.	Parent gives child permission to talk about past trauma.	NA 0 1 2 3 4
5.	Parent tells child they are willing to listen to what the child has to say.	NA 0 1 2 3 4
6.	Parent lets child know that they will not be angry with what the child has to say.	NA 0 1 2 3 4
7.	Parent listens to child's story attentively and empathetically.	NA 0 1 2 3 4
8.	Parent uses reflective listening and attending skills.	NA 0 1 2 3 4
9.	Parent asks what was the worst part of the event for the child.	NA 0 1 2 3 4
10.	Parent does not show signs of shock or repulsion.	NA 0 1 2 3 4
11.	Parent apologizes for their part in the child's trauma.	NA 0 1 2 3 4
12.	Parent accepts responsibility for their part in the child's trauma.	NA 0 1 2 3 4
13.	Parent does not place blame on the child for the trauma.	NA 0 1 2 3 4
14.	Parent explains to the child that the trauma was not the child's fault.	NA 0 1 2 3 4

SUMMARY OF HEALING GOALS

Sum of answered items = _____ "Total Score"
# of Answered items _____ x 4 = _____ "Ideal Score"

Total Score [ ] _____ = _____ %   Ideal Score [ ]

Comments: _____
_____
_____

Appendix C

**Tools from
St. Julian's Starting Over
Child Visitation Center**

STARTING OVER
SUPERVISED VISITATION

SUPERVISED VISITATION REFERRAL FORM

Please complete and Fax along with a copy of the Order to the attention of Diane Campbell. FAX NUMBER 770-949-1799

Referring Judge: _____County: _____

Name of Custodial Parent:_____

Attorney of Custodial Parent: _____

Name of Non-Custodial Parent:_____

Attorney for Non-Custodial Parent: _____

Reason For Supervised Visits: _____

_____

Days, Number of Hours & Frequency of Visits: _____

_____

Who, other than non-custodial parent is allowed at the visits: _____

_____

Special Instructions / Restrictions during visits: _____

_____

_____

Sent By: _____ Phone: _____Date: _____

% St. Julian's Episcopal Church, 5400 Stewart Mill Rd, Douglasville, Ga 30135 . 770-949-9949

RULES FOR SUCCESSFUL VISITS

This is a volunteer service, therefore we reserve the right to withdraw services, end visits, and contact law enforcement if any of the following rules are violated or restrictions noted by the referring judge are committed, depending on the severity of the violation and the threat to the safety of the child(ren). We are offering this services because we are aware of the desperate need for a safe place for children to visit their non-custodial parent. This service is for the children.

The custodial parent is asked:
> -To deliver the child(ren) 15 minutes prior to the visit;
> -To return for pick up of your child promptly when the visit is scheduled to end and enter the facility through the side door where you will be escorted to a waiting area;
> -No contact with the non-custodial parent on grounds.

The non-custodial parent is asked:
> -To arrive for visits promptly when the visit is scheduled to begin and enter through the front door of the facility;
> -To begin saying goodby to your child(ren) 5 minutes before the visit is to end, and be prepared to leave promptly when the visit is to end.
> -Come prepared for the visit.
> -No contact with the custodial parent on the grounds.

-Neither party is to loiter in the church parking lot or the church property;
-No physical or verbal abuse will be tolerated;
-Any restriction noted by the judge will be closely monitored. Violations will end the visit for that day;
-Should either parent be noticeably intoxicated or "high," law enforcement will be notified immediately. Further, should the non-custodial parent be intoxicated or "high," there will be no visit.
-Should the custodial parent not deliver or pick up the child on the date and time designated, the non-custodial parent's attorney, and/or the judge, and if involved, the Department of Family and Children's Services will be notified.
-There will be brief notes taken on all facets of the visit and available to the attending attorneys and judge.

SUPERVISED VISITATION RELEASE FORM
Custodial Parent

I,_____ request Saint Julian's Episcopal Church's Supervised

Visitation Program to provide supervision of visits for my child(ren),

specifically,_____

to visit with their (father/mother) _____

I understand that information concerning these visits will be available to the non-custodial

parent's attorney, and :

My attorney (name, phone#)_____

Child(rens) attorney (name, phone#)_____

Superior Court Judge_____

Juvenile Judge_____

Other_____

    I further understand that St. Julian's reserves the right to report to Family and Children's Services any abuse and/or neglect suspected.

    I have read and understand the "Rules for a Successful Visit." I understand that should the rules be violated that the Supervisors have the right to cancel that specific visit and/or all future visits at their discretion.

    I agree that should a visit be canceled before the visitation time has ended I can be reached at _____and will come promptly to pick up my child(ren).

    I agree to deliver my child(ren) to St. Julian's 15 minutes prior to the agreed upon visitation time, and will return 5 minutes past the visitation time to pick up my child(ren). I further agree not to have any direct contact with their father/mother on church grounds.

    I understand St. Julian's Episcopal Church is providing these services as a ministry to this community. I come to Saint Julian's requesting they supervise these visits free of charge. I hereby release them of any liabilities, including, but not limited to, injuries, kidnap, or theft.

_____   _____
    (Signature)   (Date)   (Witness)   (Date)

_____   _____
    Name printed   Name Printed

Appendix D

Tools from the
Family Visitation Center

Director
David A. Berns

Deputy Director
Barbara Drake

**Dept. of
Human Services
El Paso County**

"Strengthening the Family and Community"

**Board of County
Commissioners**
Charles C. Brown
Duncan S. Bremer
Jeri Howells
Betty Beedy
Ed Jones

FAMILY VISITATION CENTER RULES

The following rules help assure you and your children have pleasant and beneficial visits.

General

_____ Visits are documented, even cancellations; call and communicate reasons for missed visits.

_____ The Family Visitation Center is a smoke free environment.

_____ Additional parties are not allowed at the FVC without the caseworker and FVC approval.

_____ No make-up visitation for court appointments, holidays, or parent canceled visits.

_____ Proper self-hygiene is required – shoes, and shirt must be worn at all times.

_____ For you and your children, you must be alcohol and drug free. If there is an odor of alcohol you will be asked to leave the center.

_____ Reasonable requests by the Family Visitation Center staff are expected to be followed.

Arrival

_____ Arrive 10-15 minutes early for your scheduled visitation to greet your children.

_____ Your visitation will be canceled if you are not here within 15 minutes after your scheduled visitation time.

_____ Park in front of the center on El Paso or Boulder streets and enter and exit by the front door.

_____ Sign-in and wait in the reception area.

_____ Bring in all your supplies for visitation at once. Do not come in and out of the center.

Visits

_____ Bring all supplies needed for your visit. This includes food for meals or snacks, formula, diapers, change of clothes, toys or activities (bake cookies, prepare snack together, make crafts, dye Easter eggs, etc.…).

_____ You can photograph your children, but do not take pictures of other parents or children visiting at the center.

_____ When it is dark and cold outside visitations must remain inside.

_____ Clean up each area before moving to a new one. Please be aware of other visits.

_____ Conversations should be positive. Answer questions but do not be negative about the situation or discuss legal matters with your children.

_____ Reception area is not for visitation. Once you have greeted your children move on to a visitation area for activity and interaction with your children.

_____ Spend entire time with your children. Do not make telephone calls or visits with friends.

_____ Food is allowed in dining areas or outside <u>only</u> - absolutely no red or grape drinks in center.

_____ No physical punishment or verbal abuse is allowed. Use "time-outs - or redirect your child as needed. Feel free to ask staff members for help.

_____ Teach children proper respect for their bodies. Use age appropriate touch and boundaries.

_____ The goodbye should be fast and positive. It must be done inside the center. Parents are not to accompany their children to the parking area.

SIGNATURE:_____   DATE:_____

105 North Spruce   P.O. Box 2692   Colorado Springs, Colorado 80901   719.636.0000   Fax: 719.444.5599

Family Visitation Center Request for Services

Caseworker_____   Referral Date _____

Case Name _____   Initial Case Opening _____

Child Placement Agency _____   Worker Phone Number _____

DHS Monitor _____   Monitor Phone Ext. _____

Unit:

☐ **EPP** - Please submit the Intake Summary, FSP with Treatment and Visitation Plan if available.

☐ **CWI/ACIT** - Please submit Intake Summary or Initial FSP if available.

☐ **On-going Protective** - Please submit Transfer Summary and FSP.

☐ **On-going Youth and Family Services** - Please submit Transfer Summary or FSP.

Child's Name	Age	Sex	Placement	Phone	Visitors	Relationship to Child	Phone

Goals you would like to have implemented during visitation.

1. _____

_____

2. _____

_____

Please describe in detail the level of supervision expected. _____

_____

_____

_____

Desired frequency and duration of visits. _____

Is there a Court Ordered Schedule? ____ Yes ____ No

Dept. of Human Services
El Paso County

Child Visitation Plan

Child's Name _____ Age _____

Parent's Names _____

Date of Staffing _____ Caseworker _____

Child's Placement _____

1. Child's Developmental Level:
   _____ A. On target   _____ C. Delayed for age
   _____ B. Advanced for age   _____ D. Unsure at this time

2. Child's Adjustment to foster placement: _____
   _____
   _____

3. Reason for specific placement with regard to provider's ability to meet child's needs: _____
   _____
   _____
   _____

4. Reason visits need to be supervised at FVC: _____
   _____
   _____

5. Contact occurring with siblings? _____

6. Contact occurring with extended family? _____

7. Child's Permanency Plan at this time: _____

8. Approximate time period of FVC involvement: _____

9. Is parent required to attend parenting or nurturing classes? _____

   _____ Physical Abuse   _____ Emotional Abuse

   _____ Sexual Abuse   _____ Nutritional

   _____ Neglect   _____ Drug/Alcohol

   _____ Physical   _____ Domestic Violence

Visitation Schedule _____
   _____
   _____

Next Progress Review _____

Caseworker Signature _____

FVC Staff Signature _____

Household Number _____

Appendix E

Tools from Neighborhood Foster Care

BIRTH PARENTS
Bridging the Gap of Separation with Their Children
• A Continuum of Contact •
Developed by the Department of Children and Family Services, County of Cuyahoga, Ohio

• Send cards and letters to child at foster home via social worker • Send family pictures to child via social worker • Attend all visits and meetings • Attend all classes and appointments • Make regular contact with social worker • Plan special activities for visits • Remember child's birthday and holidays • Talk with child about separation • Write down important information about child such as diet, routine, habits, etc. • Send medical/school, etc. records to foster parent via social worker • Encourage child to cooperate with placement • Share critical cultural information with foster parent	• Discuss child's activities with foster parent at visits • Share family information with foster parent • Arrange phone calls from child • Develop positive relationship with foster parent • Talk with foster parent at agency meetings • Give foster parent your home phone number • Attend school meetings with foster parent • Help develop the child's lifebook • Include foster parent in visitation activities • Do not make unrealistic promises to child • Avoid giving child a specific date for reunification • Learn about, understand, and respect the foster parent's culture	• Invite foster parent to your home • Phone child at foster home • Invite foster parent to child's birthday party • Discuss case plan progress with foster parent • Review child's behavior with foster parent • Invite foster parent to attend parenting classes with you • Ask foster parent for help in locating community resources • Include foster parent in child's return home	• Visit child in foster home • Work with foster parent on discipline problems • Call foster parent for help with parenting problems • Assist child with keeping in contact with foster parent after reunification • Work with foster parent to solve school problems • Include foster parent in holiday celebrations • Show appreciation to foster parent • Offer to take child to appointments for foster parent

FOSTER PARENTS
Bridging the Gap of Separation Between Children and Their Families
• A Continuum of Contact •
Developed by the Department of Children and Family Services, County of Cuyahoga, Ohio

• Exchange letters with child's family • Call child's parent on phone • Request pictures of child's family • Give parents pictures of child • Share copies of homework and report cards with family • Have positive view of child's family • Send snack/activity for visit • Encourage parent's progress • Dress child up for visits • Share monthly progress reports with birth parent • Host and arrange sibling visits • Brag to parent about child • Request cultural information from birth parent	• Transport child to visit • Talk with parent at visit • Encourage parent to phone child • Meet child's family at placement • Have a nonthreatening attitude • Refer to child as "your child" • Share parenting information • Attend staffings and reviews • Help birth parents find community resources • Encourage and reassure reunifications • Share child's life book with parents • Attend training to learn how to work directly with birth parents • Learn about, understand, and respect the birth parent's culture	• Take/pickup child to/at parent's home • Serve as parent's mentor • Review child's visits with parent • Give parents verbal progress reports • Ask parent to come to appointments • Transport birth parents to meetings • Invite child's family to attend school programs • Assist in planning child's return to birth home	• Welcome child's parents into your home • Attend parenting classes with parents • Arrange family visits with parents • Serve as support for family following reunification • Provide respite care for birth family • Include birth parents in farewell activities

SOCIAL WORKERS
Bridging the Gap of Separation Between Children and Their Families
• A Continuum of Contact •
Developed by the Department of Children and Family Services, County of Cuyahoga, Ohio

• Encourage info exchange between birth/foster parents • Have birth/foster parents exchange pictures • Talk positively about birth families to foster families • Schedule regular, frequent visits • Share all information with foster/birth parents • Encourage foster parents to host sibling visits • Serve as liaison between foster/birth families • Describe foster parents in nonidentifying terms at placement • Exchange monthly progress reports with birth/foster parents • Serve as positive role model to foster/birth parents • Assist foster/birth families in understanding cultural differences	• Ensure that foster/birth parents attend agency meetings • Facilitate conversations between birth/foster families • Have foster/birth parents meet at placement • Encourage foster/birth families to work on life book together • Encourage birth parents to permit foster parents to call home • Set clear boundaries for contact • Facilitate the development of a collaborative relationship between birth parents and foster parents • Debrief foster parents regarding birth parents' problems/needs • Participate in visitations • Talk openly with birth/foster parents about their concerns • Help foster parents understand the birth parents' problems	• Assist birth parents in welcoming foster parents to home • Encourage foster parent to transport child to home • Permit foster parents to invite birth parents to attend all appointments • Encourage foster parents to transport birth parents to agency meetings and child's appointments • Assist foster parents and birth parents in managing conflict • Mediate and resolve conflicts	• Assist foster parents in welcoming birth parents to home • Allow foster parents and birth parents to schedule all visitation • Encourage post-reunification contact • Suggest that foster parents can provide respite care after reunification • Discuss how foster parents can serve as support to birth parents • Empower foster parents to set limits and boundaries regarding contact and visitation

Cultural Responsiveness Checklist

- Place Neighborhood Foster Care (NFC) children in homes that most resemble their cultural and language backgrounds.

- Make every attempt to provide same language services to children and their families.

- Provide translated NFC materials to meet the language need of families participating in the program.

- Promote, develop, and provide cultural diversity education to all NFC participants and staff.

- Contact NFC staff if there is a question regarding the cultural resources NFC provides.

- Provide training and education for NFC participants to learn about cultural back grounds of people in their communities.

- Enlist support and services by culturally appropriate providers within neighborhoods.

- Have culturally appropriate systems for quality assurance and continuous quality improvement.

Visitation Checklist

- Visitations are arranged by agreement between the foster family, kinship provider, birth family, and family advocate.

- Caseworkers are notified of all visitations by the foster family or kinship provider.

- A simple log is filled out by the foster family or community resource worker. This log documents the quality, frequency, and dynamics of the visit.

- If transportation is needed, the community resource worker or the family advocate should be contacted.

- If child care is required, the community resource worker arranges for child care or arranges for compensation for child care from SCF for the foster family or kinship provider.

- Whenever possible, visitations are held at NFC sites or community sites that are friendly, comfortable, and accessible.

- Visitations can include meal preparation by the birth parent. Birth parents are encouraged to accompany their child and the foster parent to medical appointments, attend school functions or teacher conferences, share meals with the child and foster parent in local restaurants, and attend recreational activities.

- If supervision is required by the court, NFC assures all rules are met while maintaining a child and family friendly approach to visitation.

Appendix F

**Tools from the
California Professional Society
on the Abuse of Children**

Purpose

Family reunification is one of the legislatively mandated goals of the California Dependency Court. After allegations of sexual abuse or a sustained petition, an appropriate plan can assist the Court in reunifying the family in a timely and successful manner. Premature or poorly planned visitation can impede a family's reunification process. The rights of families are best served by a coordinated visitation and reunification plan

A goal of Family Court is to assist families with children to transition in the best possible manner to a different family structure. When there are allegations of sexual abuse in Family Court proceedings, the safety of the child is essential to maintain while providing for the rights of the parents.

This document is offered to assist decisionmakers, in cases when sexual abuse allegations appear reasonably credible in Family Court or there is a prima facie case in Dependency Court, to determine when monitored visits should be ordered.

This document was written by a multidisciplinary task force of the California Professional Society on the Abuse of Children (CAPSAC). It is an update of a document produced in 1993 by a task force of the CAPSAC-L.A. Board.

Comments, suggestions, and questions should be directed to the chairperson, Toni Cavanagh Johnson, Ph.D., 1101 Fremont Ave., Suite 101, South Pasadena, CA 91030, Tel: 626-799-4522, Fax: 818-790-0139, e-mail: TCavJohn@aol.com.

The following are guidelines and are not intended to serve as a rigid blueprint for practice nor are they intended to establish a legal standard to which professionals must adhere. Rather, the guidelines provide a model of desirable professional practice.

A. Important Points Related to Monitored Visits

1. What happens in the initial contacts between an (alleged) child victim and an (alleged) perpetrator after allegations of sexual abuse have come to light is central to their ongoing relationship and future healthy reunification. A step-wise process is in the best interest of the child. (See Section B and Charts I and II, pages 178–179.)

2. Bonding occurs within the first days and hours of a child's relationship to his or her parents. The attachment relationship between a parent and child develops over the lifetime of a child. A period of investigation resulting from allegations of abuse will not disrupt a healthy attachment between a parent and a child.

3. It is well established that child abuse has at its core the issue of the power and influence of the perpetrator over the victim. While monitored visits prevent the continuation of the physical activity of the sexually abusive relationship of the perpetrator to the victim, monitoring may not forestall the emotionally abusive relationship. Emotional abuse and sexual intrusion are the hallmarks of sexual abuse. The emotional damage of sexual abuse far outlasts any physical damage.

4. A child who has been allegedly abused may require a period of time to feel protected, to understand each person's responsibility related to abuse, and to develop self-protection skills prior to visiting the (alleged) abuser. Some reasons abused children may want immediate visits with the person that allegedly abused them include the following: (a) see if the person is angry, (b) ask for forgiveness for making the allegations, (c) get gifts, (d) assuage other family member's anger at the (alleged) victim, (e) express their love and caring for the person, and (f) see if the person is all right.

5. The influence of a perpetrator on a child victim during visitations is substantial. A monitor may not recognize the perpetrator's influence on the child. A child can be influenced by the physical movements, glances, smell, or clothing of an offender, which may trigger traumatic memories. Certain foods, toys, books, or other things brought by the perpetrator may have strong negative connotations for the child or be subtle reminders of the emotionally controlling aspects of the relationship from which the child struggled to get away. The offender's influence may eventuate in the child recanting the allegations. A child may not feel supported, believed or that allegations of sexual abuse are serious if, without preparation, he or she simply starts visits and telephone calls with the person by whom he or she was (allegedly) abused. A process needs to occur before visits begin. (See Section B and Charts I and II, pages 178–179.)

6. Because premature visits of offenders with their victims impedes the perpetrator's progress in treatment, Senate Bill 3560 was sponsored by the California Coalition on Sexual Offending, a multidisciplinary group of service providers to sexual offenders. Section 1202.05 and 5154.2 of the California Penal Code now state that incarcerated offenders may not have visits with their victims who are under 18 years of age. The Director of Corrections will only allow visits when the Juvenile Court, pursuant to sections 362.6 of the Welfare and Institutions Code, finds that such visits are in the best interest of the child.

7. The parental alienation syndrome applies in custody disputes when no abuse has occurred and one parent overtly or covertly vilifies the other parent to a child, who thereafter deprecates that parent.

Parental alienation is not a valid issue when a parent has been sexually, physically or emotionally abusive (per Richard Gardner, M.D.). The concept is often misinterpreted and misapplied to the anger and distrust a child, as well as the nonmolesting parent, evidences toward an abusive parent. In cases where the nonmolesting parent is protective of the abused child/ren, anger at the (alleged) perpetrator is natural. In cases where the nonmolesting parent's allegiance is to the (alleged) perpetrator and not the (alleged) victim, the child victim's mental health is in jeopardy.

B. The Decision to Order Therapeutic Contacts, Eventuating in Monitored Visits

1. Chart 1 (page 178) provides a schematic of the process involved in deciding when to order visits in the Dependency Court. Chart II (page 179) provides a schematic of the process involved in deciding when to order visits in Family Court.

2. There should be no visits ordered until child protective services, mental health workers, family court services, or expert panel member have submitted a report for the review of the judicial officer. The report (Section C) will indicate when it is in the best interest of the child to have visits with the (alleged) perpetrator.

3. When available, the child and (alleged) perpetrator should have separate contact with mental health professionals in the interim between the allegations and the beginning of the visits. Included in the treatment goals is preparing the child and (alleged) perpetrator for therapeutic contact. (See Section D.)

4. The first visits ordered are for therapeutic contact. It is expected that a mental health professional, child protective services worker, or evaluator who knows both the (alleged) perpetrator and child will be present at the initial therapeutic contacts. The meetings should be held in the child therapist's office or a neutral location.

Therapeutic contact differs substantially from monitored visits. During therapeutic contacts the person guiding the contact actively engages in assisting the (alleged) perpetrator and the child to reengage in a relationship. In these therapeutic contacts, the professionals assist in: (a) discussing the allegations; (b) discussing issues of adult responsibility when abuse occurs; (c) discussing any secrets, threats, or other pressure felt by the child; (d) defining the altered relationship between the child and parent regarding physical contact during visits (See attached CAPSAC Guidelines for MonitoredVisits, pages 180–189); (e) discussing areas of concern for the child and the (alleged) perpetrator, past, present, and future; (f) talking about emotional, sexual, and physical boundaries; (g) setting the stage for future open communication; and (h) assisting in any helpful dialogue between the parties.

During therapeutic contacts the child is supported in what he or she wishes to say to the (alleged) perpetrator regarding the allegations or other matters. The (alleged) perpetrator need not acknowledge any statements made by the child regarding the allegations (if the allegations have been denied) but is asked to listen to and not contradict or question the child. The child is told that the (alleged) perpetrator will listen even if he or she disputes the child's veracity. This session is not used to determine the truth of allegations, and all parties should have this explained ahead of time. (See CAPSAC Guidelines for Monitored Visits, pages 180–189.)

This therapeutic contact is supportive of the child and is used to provide understanding of the relationship between the child and the (alleged) perpetrator and to state the reasons for the court requirement of monitoring.

Without discussion regarding the allegations of abuse, a child victim may develop self-defeating behavior repeatedly seen in battered spouses. Battered spouses can engage in a continuous cycle of returning to the batterer with neither partner adequately acknowledging the abuse, only to leave and return again after subsequent abusive incidents.

5. Therapeutic contacts will give way to suitably monitored visits unless the outcome of these initial contacts contraindicates such visits. In that case, the professionals assisting in the therapeutic contacts will make recommendations to the court regarding further preparations of the child and the (alleged) perpetrator for healthy contacts.

6. A suitable monitor is a professional monitor or someone known and trusted by the child, who believes the court was correct to order monitored visits and is willing and capable of protecting the minor, that is, has adequate assertion skills and influence over the (alleged) perpetrator that he or she will conform to the rules of the visits as imposed by the monitor. (See CAPSAC Guidelines for Monitored Visits, pages 180–189.)

C. Information Required from Mental Health Professionals/Child Protective Services/Family Court Services/Expert Panel Members to Assist in Determining When to Begin Therapeutic Contacts

1. Report on Child

(a) Is the child clear about issues related to responsibility when an adult molests a child?

(b) Can the child talk about the (alleged) sexual abuse without significant anxiety, shame, or guilt? Will the child be able to state his or her feelings to the (alleged) perpetrator? If not, can the child listen while a mental health professional talks about the (alleged) abuse to the (alleged) perpetrator in order to set the stage for the visits?

(c) If the child is highly sexualized, will meeting with the (alleged) perpetrator exacerbate the condition?

(d) What are the child's feelings about visiting the (alleged) perpetrator? What statements has the child made? Is the child allowed by the nonmolesting parent to experience his or her own emotions regarding the allegations and the (alleged) offender? Are the child's feelings about meeting with the (alleged) perpetrator unduly influenced by the needs of the nonmolesting parent or other family members?

(e) Is the child likely to be highly distressed by the visits? If so, will this be detrimental to the child's emotional health?

(f) If the child wants to visit with the (alleged) perpetrator, who will be present to assist the child in talking about the (alleged) abuse and other relevant issues? This could be the child's therapist, counselor, or social worker. The person must be someone with whom the child is comfortable and who can speak about the (alleged) abuse in a therapeutic manner.

(g) Does the (alleged) perpetrator play an integral role in the developing mental health of the child? What has been the quality of the attachment between the child and the (alleged) perpetrator? Is the child going to suffer from not visiting with the (alleged) perpetrator? If the child wants to visit with the (alleged) perpetrator, are the child's motivations in the best interests of his or her recovery from the (alleged) abusive relationship? In what way will the child profit from the visit?

(h) Are there any concerns about the victim's relationship to siblings, the nonmolesting parent, or extended family members? Are safety measures necessary for contact of the (alleged) victim with other family members?

(i) Provide future treatment goals, a proposed timetable for resuming contact, and any other information that will help the judicial officer make the decision about when to begin therapeutic contact between the child and (alleged) perpetrator.

2. Report on (Alleged) Perpetrator

(a) With the understanding that there is no requirement to agree or appear to agree with the allegations, will the (alleged) perpetrator allow the child or the mental health professional working with the child to freely discuss the allegations or contents of a sustained petition in the initial therapeutic contact?

(b) If the child has said "no" to visits, is the (alleged) perpetrator able to understand the child's apprehension or concerns?

(c) Is the (alleged) perpetrator acting in a retaliatory manner or demanding his or her rights to visits, regardless of the child's statements and/or emotional and behavioral condition?

(d) How much progress has the (alleged) perpetrator made in being able to understand and act on behalf of the best interests of the child? Is the (alleged) perpetrator ready to behave in a way that will enrich, rather than potentially further harm, the child's relationship to him or her?

(e) What is the level of insight of the (alleged) perpetrator? Does the (alleged) perpetrator take responsibility for any negative or problematic behaviors toward the child and/or other people significant to the child?

(f) Does the (alleged) perpetrator understand ways in which people may violate the emotional, sexual, and physical space of the child? Can the (alleged) perpetrator articulate what the child alleges happened? If the (alleged) perpetrator denies the (alleged) sexual abuse, can he or she discuss abuse issues hypothetically, that is, how might a sexually abused child feel?

(g) Does the (alleged) perpetrator understand and agree to follow the rules regarding physical contact and verbal interactions with the child during the therapeutic contacts and monitored visits? (See CAPSAC Guidelines for Monitored Visits, pages 180–189.) Does the (alleged) perpetrator see people's need for physical and emotional space and boundaries?

(h) If the (alleged) offender blames the nonmolesting parent for the allegations, can he or she see the need to forego this battle with the other parent when interacting with the child?

(i) Provide future treatment goals, a proposed timetable for resuming contact, and any other information that will help the judicial officer make the decision about when to begin therapeutic contact between the child and (alleged) perpetrator.

3. Report on the Nonmolesting Parent

(a) Is the nonmolesting parent sufficiently aware of how the (alleged) abusive relationship was able to occur without detection? Has the nonmolesting parent become aware of and assumed responsibility for whatever part he or she may have played in the (alleged) abuse?

(b) Describe the nonmolesting parent's assignment of blame for the abuse. How does the nonmolesting parent see the role/function of each family member in the (alleged) abuse?

(c) How have the nonmolesting parent and the family adjusted subsequent to the allegations or the sustained petition of sexual abuse? Are there adequate protections in place for nonmolested siblings?

(d) Is the nonmolesting parent adequately prepared to support the child and transport the child to therapeutic contacts with the (alleged) perpetrator?

(e) If the child's therapist believes the child is ready to begin therapeutic sessions with the (alleged) perpetrator, is the nonmolesting parent in agreement? If not, describe the issues and what movement is being made toward their resolution.

(f) If the child is outside the home and the (alleged) perpetrator and nonmolesting parent are living together or friendly, how does this affect the initial therapeutic interactions? Who should be present? Is the nonmolesting parent sufficiently protective of the (alleged) child victim and other siblings?

(g) What are the nonmolesting parent's feelings about the (alleged) victim visiting the (alleged) perpetrator? What statements has the nonmolesting parent made? Is the child allowed by the nonmolesting parent to experience his or her own emotions regarding the allegations and the (alleged) offender? Are the child's feelings about meeting with the (alleged) perpetrator unduly influenced by the needs of the nonmolesting parent or other family members?

(h) Provide future treatment goals, a proposed timetable for resuming contact, and any other information that will help the judicial officer make the decision about when to begin therapeutic contact between the child and (alleged) perpetrator.

4. Report on the Minor's Caretaker (if not the nonmolesting parent)

(a) If the child's therapist believes the child is ready to begin therapeutic sessions with the (alleged) perpetrator, is the child's caretaker in agreement?

(b) Is the child's caretaker adequately prepared to support the child and transport the child to therapeutic contacts with the (alleged) perpetrator? If not, provide a proposed plan for preparing for the visits.

5. Report for Child Protective Services (if applicable)

(a) Describe the role and goals of all therapists and other community supports working with family members.

(b) Provide the results of CPS assessment of all family members. Are there other victims in the family? How are the siblings of the (alleged) victim reacting to the allegations and to their sibling?

(c) Include as attachments letters from all the therapists involved with any family members. If there are no other mental health providers, the CPS worker should answer the questions outlined in Section C 1-4.

(d) Make recommendations regarding when it is in the best interest of the child to start therapeutic contact leading to monitored visitation for the (alleged) child victim.

(e) Make recommendations regarding visitation for the siblings of the (alleged) victim.

(f) Suggest an appropriate treatment plan and case plan for the family.

(g) In the event that there are no auxiliary therapeutic professionals, the CPS worker should propose an alternate means of proceeding with therapeutic contact, monitored visits and eventual family reunification.

D. Therapy for the Parties

1. If the (alleged) perpetrator due to denial of the allegations is not in sex offender specific therapy, he or she should be in therapy working on: (a) an empathetic response to his or her child's belief regarding the (sustained) allegations; (b) preparation for monitored visits; (c) impulse control, problem solving, and conflict resolution; (d) understanding healthy physical and emotional relationships between adults, and between adults and children; (e) the dynamic of sexual abuse and its effects on the child/victim, siblings, nonmolesting parent, and family unit; (f) developmentally appropriate parenting roles and responsibilities related to child/victims and siblings; (g) healthy emotional, physical, and sexual boundaries between adults and children; and (h) if the (alleged) perpetrator thinks all fault for the allegations lies with the nonmolesting parent, how he or she plans to control this when with the (alleged) victim.

2. The nonmolesting parent generally requires a separate therapist from the child to assure that any competing needs of the nonmolesting parent and the child are accurately identified and worked through.

The role of the nonmolesting parent is important in the reunification of the family. If the nonmolesting parent is supportive of the child, regular contact with this parent in preparation for successful reunification will be important. If not supportive of the child, all visits should be closely monitored.

3. Mental health professionals who work with the (alleged) perpetrator, nonmolesting parent, siblings, and the (alleged) victim should be ordered to be in regular contact with one another throughout the therapy process. (The task force is aware that if there are parallel proceedings in Criminal Court that the psychotherapist-patient privilege may be at issue.) Regular contact with child protective services is also essential, if they are involved.

E. Charts I and II (Pages 178–179)

1. These charts reflect the suggested decisionmaking process for ordering visitation in cases where allegations of sexual abuse appear reasonably credible in Family Court or there is a prima facie case in Dependency Court. The pertinent sections of this document are referred to in the charts.

Chart I

Decisionmaking Process for Ordering Visitation When There is a Prima Facie Case of Sexual Abuse in Dependency Cases

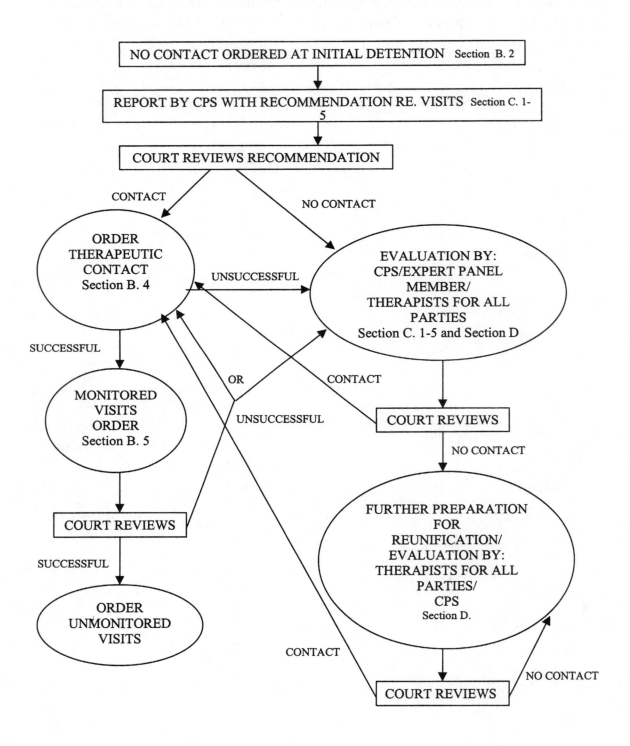

Chart II

Decisionmaking Process for Ordering Visitation When Sexual Abuse Allegations Appear Reasonably Credible in Family Law Cases

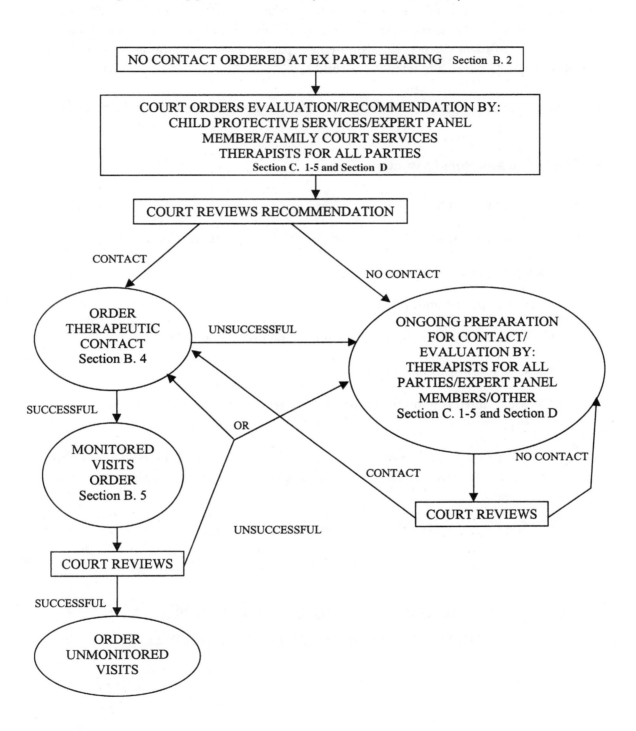

Location of Monitoring

- **Open Monitored Visitation**

The location can be chosen by the person being monitored with the consent of the monitor. Choices would include parks, malls, relative's home, playgrounds, restaurants, hotel rooms for out- of-town visitors, etc. (Amusement parks, movies, swimming pools and spas are difficult places to provide safety for a child.)

There may be transportation between locations. The monitor should always be with the child.

- **Single Site Monitored Visitation**

  - Monitored in parent's home

  - Location selected by person being monitored with agreement of the monitor

  - Monitor's place of business

    - Open area or multiple rooms

    - One room with monitor viewing through one-way mirror

    - One room with monitor in room

      Most suited to monitoring when there are allegations of abuse under investigation

      Most suited to monitoring when abuse has occurred and the perpetrator and the victim have not yet had therapeutic contact in which the abuse has been discussed

      Most suited when there are concerns about abduction

**MONITORED VISITS SHOULD NOT BE IN PLACES
CHILD ALLEGES ABUSE TO HAVE OCCURRED.**

Guidelines for Visiting Party

Section 1

- The time and length of the visits must be pre-arranged and only rarely changed.

- Directions given by the monitor must be followed. No discussion of the rules with the child present.

- There should be no attempt to get the monitor to side with anyone. The monitor must remain impartial.

- Child must be within the monitor's hearing and sight at all times.

- No use of foreign language or words unfamiliar to the monitor.

- No whispering, passing notes, or hand signals. No swearing or cuss words.

- No negative comments about the other parent, caretaker, child, or child's siblings.

- No discussion of the court case, social worker, or related matters, such as visitation restrictions.

- *No tickling, hugging, kissing, or holding, unless freely initiated by the child.

- **The visiting person (if an adult) is responsible for managing the child's behavior. No spanking, hitting, or threatening. The monitor will help, if needed.

- Unless previously agree upon, the visiting person will be the only person allowed into the visit.

- No visits while the visiting person appears to be under the influence of alcohol or illegal drugs.

- No loud talk, name-calling, or ridiculing. No questioning, which makes the child uncomfortable.

- Visiting persons should try not to appear lonely or needy. This may cause child to worry or feel guilty.

- The monitor or child is not to be used to communicate with the other parent/caretaker.

- No promises like "you'll live with me soon (go to Disneyland)," unless already agreed on by the court.

- No prolonged or tearful good-byes.

Section 2. Additional Guidelines if there are Allegations of Sexual Abuse

Without prior approval of the court, child's therapist and/or the child's protective services worker:

- No exchange of gifts, money, food, or cards.

- No exchange or taking of photographs, videotapes, or audiotapes.

- *No physical contact with the child such as lap sitting, combing hair or stroking any other part of the body, hand holding, arm around the shoulders, prolonged hugging, wrestling, horse-playing, tickling, changing diapers, or accompanying the child to the bathroom, even if requested by the child.

- **If there is a sustained petition of sexual abuse or a criminal conviction of sexual abuse against the visiting party, that person will not be responsible for managing the behavior of the child. The monitor or another visiting adult will do it.

The monitor may terminate the visit at any time if the above guidelines are violated, or if any other behavior occurs that the monitor deems inappropriate, or the child appears unduly distressed. This document can serve as the basis of an incident report. When the person being monitored does not follow the guidelines, it will be reported to the court or the supervising authorities.

I have read the rules and agree to follow those checked in Section 1:_____

I have read the rules and agree to follow those checked in Section 1 and 2: _____

Visiting Person's Signature:_____ **Date:**_____

Monitor's Signature:_____ **Date:**_____

Suggestions for Visiting Persons

1. If therapeutic contact is ordered by the court, a session or sessions will assist you and the child to gain an understanding regarding the court's decision to require supervision. The child will be encouraged to discuss his or her understanding of the reason for the therapeutic contact and anything else that is on the child's mind. The supervisor of the session will state to the child that you will listen whether you agree or not with some or all of what the child alleges. If the child has made allegations of abuse or maltreatment and you dispute them, you are asked only to listen to the child, if he or she brings them up. This is not a fact-finding session. It is not expected that you agree to any allegations you dispute, yet you are not to dispute them with the child or in front of the child.

2. These visits are for the benefit of you and the child. The monitor is to assist to make the visit safe and pleasant. Please be on time. Call _____, the monitor, at _____ (tel. no.) if you will have to miss a visit. Please call 24 hours in advance. This will provide the monitor adequate notice and the child will not be disappointed at the last minute. The visits will occur on a regularly scheduled basis, unless otherwise ordered. Except in extraordinary circumstances, canceled visits will not be rescheduled.

3. Encourage the child with statements such as, "You did a good job." "Wow, you are learning new things." "Great." "I am proud of you." "You are taking turns nicely."

4. You may want to bring toys with which the child likes to play. Bring toys that will evoke positive memories, no toys that remind the child of any hurtful situations. Remember to take them home with you. No gifts, money, food, or cards are allowed if there are allegations of abuse, without approval of the court, the child's therapist, or a protective service worker. Plan some games or activities that the child will enjoy doing with you.

5. Keep a positive attitude. The conversation should be as upbeat as possible. Children should not worry about their parents' problems.

6. Be open to any feelings your child may share with you. If the child says, "You make me angry," you can reply, "I am sorry I do that." If the child says, "I hate you," you can say, "I am sorry you hate me." While you may want to contradict the child, try not to as this stops communication.

If you do not know what to say when the child expresses a feeling, you can repeat the feeling back. If the child says, "You make me angry," you can say "I make you angry." If the child says, "I hate you," you can say, "you hate me." What is important is the tone of voice. You repeat the feeling in a thoughtful manner that does not deny the feelings the child is expressing.

If you want to encourage the child to tell you more about the feeling you can say, "I make you angry?" or "How do I make you angry?" In reply to "I hate you," you can say, "You hate me?" or "What do I do that makes you hate me?" These statements should be said in a calm and interested manner that encourages the child to talk about the feeling.

7. Be sensitive to the child's needs and feelings. Children like it when an adult picks up on their feelings. If the child looks scared, you can say,"Are you feeling scared?" If the child is not interested in the current activity you can say, "Is there something else you would rather do?"

8. Be supportive of the person taking care of your child. At the end of the visit say, "Have a good time with _____. I will see you in _____days."

9. Follow GUIDELINES FOR MONITORED VISITS so that the visit will proceed without any interruptions and everyone will be comfortable.

10. If you feel uncomfortable with any behaviors or guidelines of the monitor, please talk to the monitor before or after the visit, not in front of the child or person transporting the child.

Guidelines for Persons Transporting Child to and from Monitored Visits

What you say to the child prior to turning him or her over to the monitor can assist the child to feel safe and secure. It will help if you say something like "This is Sally (monitor), have a good time. She will keep you safe during your visit. I will see you _____(give location) after the visit."

- The time and length of the visits must be pre-arranged and only rarely changed.

- Child should be brought on time and go directly to the monitor to start the visit.

- No prolonged or tearful good-byes.

- Person transporting the child should not appear lonely or needy. This may cause the child to worry or feel guilty.

- There should be no attempt to get the monitor to side with anyone. The monitor must remain impartial.

- Directions given by the monitor must be followed. No discussion of the rules with child present.

- No arguing in front of the child. No swearing or curse words.

- No discussion of the court case, social worker, or related matters, such as visitation rules.

- You must not be under the influence of alcohol or illegal drugs.

- No questions or comments about child's parent/s or caretaker/s.

- No spanking, hitting, or threatening. Person transporting is responsible for managing the child when the child is with him or her.

- No use of foreign language or words unknown by the monitor.

- The monitor or child is not to be used to communicate with the other parent/caretaker.

- Child must be picked up on time.

- Encourage the child to say good-bye to all parties involved in the visit.

- Allow the child to talk about the visit. No questioning that makes the child uncomfortable.

This document can serve as the basis of an incident report. When the custodial parent or person transporting the child does not follow the rules, it will be reported to the court.

I have read and agree to follow them.

Signed:_____ **Date:**_____

Monitor's Signature:_____ **Date:**_____

Suggestions for the Monitor

It is best to meet with the visiting party prior to the day of the first visit to discuss the GUIDELINES FOR MONITORED VISITS. Be explicit and detailed in your instructions about the guidelines. Ask the visiting party to sign the GUIDELINES FOR MONITORED VISITS. If the visitor refuses, ask to which of the guidelines he or she objects. Try to understand the objections. If the majority of the guidelines are acceptable and the monitor believes the visit can be safe for the child, check the guidelines agreed upon, and have them signed. If you doubt for the safety and well being of the child, call the person or agency who requested monitoring and ask for guidance about how to proceed.

Assure that you are always within sight and hearing of the persons supervised. If you do not believe supervision of the visits is necessary, be cautious that this does not lead you to neglect the responsibility given to you by the court. Monitored visits would not have been ordered if they were not necessary.

Encourage positive interactions between the child and visiting party. This visit is to enhance the relationship between the visiting party and child.

If the parent has problems controlling the child's behavior or setting limits, assist the parent. Every attempt should be made not to embarrass the parent in front of the child. Some instruction may need to be given to the visiting party after the visit.

Be aware of visiting person trying to bribe the child with gifts or special things promised in the future.

Be aware of subtle and not so subtle messages that may confuse the child. "Mommy loves good children." "Children who go to church don't lie." "The Bible says, 'Love thy mother and father.' " "Remember the time I took you to Disneyland, would you like me to do that again?"

Be aware of signals to child that may be reminiscent of things from past interactions which told the child how to act. A nod of the head, finger pointing, winking, staring, glaring, body posture, etc.

If the monitor sees undue discomfort in the child during the visit that is not decreasing, the monitor can take the child aside and try to determine any needs the child has. If the anxiety continues and the monitor determines it is in the best interest of the child to stop the visit, this can be done.

If the visiting party will not conform to the guidelines, the visit can be terminated. Before stopping the visit give a clear message about what the visitor needs to stop or change. If after being warned the visitor will not stop, terminate the visit. Tell the child that the monitor and "visiting party will work together to make future visits work better but for now this visit will end." Document the behaviors and your warning that lead to the visit being terminated.

Write a behavioral summary of each visit. Be unbiased and objective. Do not draw conclusions unless they come directly from a balanced view of your behavioral observations. Look for positive as well as problematic behaviors.

Be aware of any negative feelings you have toward having the visit, the visitor, or the child that might impede your ability to be objective. Do not let your feelings get in the way of positive interactions between the visitor and the child. Your attitude can color the visit for all parties and color what you see and report.

Try to be aware of any cultural issues that may influence the visit.

Suggestions for Children on Monitored Visits

If the child is apprehensive about the monitored visit, a plan can be made with the child to help decrease the anxiety. (The plan can be made by the social worker and/or the therapist in conjunction with the monitor.) The child can be an active participant in order to make the visit as comfortable as possible. The plan can include any or all of the following:

- The location of the visit.

- Where everyone will sit during the visit. For instance, the child may want to be near the door or have the visitor across the room.

- What type of physical contact the child wants or does not want during the visit.

- If there are certain people the child would like or not like at the visit. (This needs to be preapproved by the social worker, therapist, and/or court depending on the court's order.)

- Hand signals that the child can use to indicate a need for help from the monitor.

- If there are things the child does not want the alleged perpetrator to bring up during the visit.

- Whether there are certain things the child wants to talk about with the alleged offender. If the child can't decide what he or she wants to say before the visit, the child can tell the monitor during the visit.

- Whether the child wants a therapist or DCFS worker to assist him or her to talk about the allegations with the alleged perpetrator prior to or during the monitored visit. (If the alleged perpetrator denies the child's allegations, he or she can be told the child wants to talk about allegations. The alleged perpetrator is not to deny the allegations nor does the alleged perpetrator need to acknowledge them.)

If the child has alleged abuse or neglect and will have visits with the alleged perpetrator, it is very helpful for the child to be able to talk openly during the visit about the allegations or for the person monitoring the visit to openly state that the reason for the monitored visits is because of the allegations. Often there is no discussion with the child about why there are to be visits after the child's allegations of abuse or after a period of separation from the alleged perpetrator. Likewise there is no mention of the allegations between the child and the alleged perpetrator. Never mentioning the allegations can lead to the child feeling unsupported or not believed, assuming that nothing really happens to someone who does bad things, and/or a belief that after a child is hurt, it is not to be discussed openly again. This can lead to behavior such as is sometimes seen in battered women who go back into abusive situations without any resolution of the abuse.

After the visits, the child can tell the monitor how the visit went and if any changes need to be made for future visits.

Appendix G

Tools from the Supervised Visitation Network

*124 14. CONDITIONS FOR PARTICIPATION IN THE SUPERVISED VISITATION PROGRAM (RULES)

Rules should be in a written form that is given to each parent and reviewed and explained. Each parent should indicate his or her understanding and acceptance of the rules by signing them in the presence of the staff person conducting the intake.

(a) The conditions for participation in the supervised visitation program (rules) should include but not be limited to the following:

i. Parties shall arrive punctually at the arranged times for the start and end of the visits.

ii. Except in an unavoidable emergency such as sudden illness, the relevant parent will inform the service as soon as possible, and at least twenty-four hours in advance, if the custodial or noncustodial parent is canceling a visit. (Repeated incidents of sudden illness may have to be verified by a licensed health provider.)

iii. Custodial and noncustodial parents agree that they (and, if applicable, authorized persons approved for inclusion in supervised visits) will remain separate, physically and visually, so that contact between them does not occur, unless there has been a specific agreement between the parties and the provider that contact may occur.

iv. Arrivals of the noncustodial and custodial parent will be at different times.

v. At the end of the visit, the noncustodial and custodial parent will have different departure times so that they may avoid contact with one another.

vi. Parties will obtain appropriate authorization before bringing an additional visitor. (See section 16.4.)

vii. No participant in the supervised visitation program may follow or harass another party before or after a scheduled supervised visit.

viii. Weapons or dangerous implements of any kind may not be brought to the supervised visitation program at any time. Participants in the supervised visitation program should be aware that security staff has a right to search them for weapons.

ix. Participants in the supervised visitation program will not use illegal substances or alcohol before or during supervised visits.

x. No client may make any threat of violence or threaten to break any court order during a supervised visit, including the transitions before and after the visit.

xi. No client may commit any violent act or break any court order during a supervised visit, including the transitions before and after the visit.

 xii. No adult may physically discipline or threaten to physically discipline a child during supervised visitation whether the locale of the visit is on- or off-site.

 xiii. A custodial parent may not make negative comments to a visiting child about the noncustodial parent, his or her partners, or family members.

 xiv. A noncustodial parent may not make negative comments to a child about the custodial parent, his or her partners, or family members.

 xv. Neither the custodial nor the noncustodial parent shall ask a child or staff member to deliver support payments or legal documents to the other parent.

 xvi. Neither the custodial nor the noncustodial parent may take any photograph or make any audio or visual recording on- or off-site during supervised visitation without prior approval of the child and the other parent.

 xvii. Written records of observations during supervised visits will be maintained and reports according to provider practice submitted to the court.

(b) Details of Visit Schedule, Additional Special Conditions

Either as part of the conditions for participation or in a separate document, for each family the following should be provided:

- frequency,
- duration,
- number of supervised visits (if known), and
- any special conditions (applying to the visits).

Custodial and noncustodial parents should make available to the provider all protective orders, including but not limited to protective orders pertaining to domestic violence and child abuse.

The above should be described in writing. These details and special conditions should be reviewed with each parent. Each parent should indicate his or her understanding and acceptance of the rules by signing them in the presence of the staff person conducting the intake.

15. INITIAL FAMILIARIZATION OF THE CHILD(REN)

15.2 Special Preparation in Cases of Family Violence

(a) If abuse of either child(ren) or a parent has been confirmed, the staff person should explain to the child in the presence of the custodial parent the safety aspects of the service provided.

(b) If there are allegations of abuse that have been denied by the visiting parent and there has been no determination of whether abuse has occurred, without going into the allegations or taking sides, the staff member should explain the safety aspects of the service provided.

(c) If there is evidence that a child has been abused or is afraid of the visiting parent, the visit supervisor should arrange a sign with the child(ren) if he or she wants the visit to end. In this prearranged way, the child(ren) can signal discomfort with less risk of angering a parent perceived as powerful and/or scary.

(d) If there is any question of physical or sexual abuse of a child, both parents and the child(ren) should be informed before the first supervised visit that physical contact is to be initiated only by the child(ren).

(e) When abuse of a child or parent has been confirmed, there should be a clearly stated acknowledgment to the child in the presence of the custodial parent that the visits will be supervised because of what the visiting parent has done and to protect the child and/or the custodial parent.

(f) When sexual abuse has been alleged and is still being evaluated, supervised visitation should not begin without consultation with the evaluator, if available, to make sure that contact between the child(ren) and the alleged abuser will not interfere with the evaluation or traumatize the child(ren).

(g) In situations involving sexual abuse of the child, whether confirmed or alleged, the non-custodial parent must not accompany the child to the bathroom or be responsible for changing diapers.

17. INTERVENTIONS DURING SUPERVISED VISITS, TERMINATING A SUPERVISED VISIT

In addition to interventions specified elsewhere in these guidelines, a visit supervisor shall stop any visit during which (a) a child becomes acutely distressed; (b) when it is deemed by the visit supervisor that the child is in a situation of possible risk either emotionally or physically; or (c) if a noncustodial parent acts in an inappropriate manner toward the child, staff, or others present. Depending on the child's reaction and the visit supervisor's assessment, stopping the visit may be a temporary interruption, with the visit resuming when the child has calmed, or the visit may be ended entirely. Terminating an individual visit shall not necessarily mean that supervised visitation services for the family shall be stopped permanently. See Section 19—Termination of Services.

20. SPECIAL CONSIDERATIONS IN SITUATIONS INVOLVING FAMILY VIOLENCE

20.1 Child Sexual Abuse

20.2 Partner Abuse

20.1 Child Sexual Abuse

(a) Any person supervising contacts between a parent and child when sexual abuse has been alleged or proved shall have specific training in child sexual abuse and shall either be a licensed or certified mental health professional, be under supervision of a licensed or certified mental health professional, have prior experience with the supervision of alleged or proven child sexual abuse, and/or have co-supervision with a trained staff person.

(b) The contact between the visiting adult and child(ren) shall be monitored continually and in a manner that allows all verbal communication between the adult and child(ren) to be heard and any physical contact to be observed.

(c) Physical contact shall be initiated only by the child and shall continue only as long as the child wants.

(d) The visit supervisor shall intervene to stop any physical contact that appears inappropriate or sexualized, even if the child does not appear distressed.

(e) The visiting adult shall not deny any statement by the child about the alleged or confirmed abuse.

(f) Because supervised visitation is not psychotherapy and because contact with an alleged or confirmed abusive adult can stir powerful emotions in a child, except when the supervision is therapeutic supervision by a licensed mental health professional, it is recommended that the child be in concurrent psychotherapy, unless or until a determination has been made by the child's therapist with the agreement of the custodial adult or by a court of competent jurisdiction that such psychotherapy is not necessary.

About the Author

Dr. Lois E. Wright is the assistant dean of the College of Social Work at the University of South Carolina and the director of The Center for Child and Family Studies. In this capacity, she has received funding for over 100 grants and contracts for research and training related to children and family services. Dr. Wright received a master of science degree in social work from the Virginia Commonwealth University and a doctorate in education from the College of William and Mary. She has more than thirty years of experience in the field of social work, and she has presented at national meetings on topics such as program evaluation, family preservation services, child neglect, and agency management.